LYRICAL LABORATORY

A COLLECTION OF POEMS FOR CHILDREN

EDITED BY ANGELA FAIRBRACE

First published in Great Britain in 2009 by:
Forward Press
Remus House
Coltsfoot Drive
Peterborough
PE2 9JX
Telephone: 01733 890099
Website: www.forwardpress.co.uk

Foreword

The job of writing poetry for children can prove
a challenging task. It requires a great deal of
imagination as well as the ability to see through a
child's eyes.

Children's poetry should not be obscure, introverted,
and as cryptic as a crossword puzzle: it is the poet's
duty to reach out and embrace the world of fantasy
that children find so fascinating.

The poems that have been selected for this
book have all captured a sense of creativity and
imagination that make them appeal to both children
and the young at heart alike. So sit back, relax and
prepare to lose yourself in a land of make-believe.

Contents

The Poems

The Jelly Monster

My name is Fred the Monster and I like to eat green jelly
I have huge eyes, a monstrous nose and a great, big, dangling belly.
My friends and I have jelly parties Thursday afternoons,
We fill a bath with the wobbly stuff and eat it with huge spoons.

Tuesdays, I like walking and I like to hear the sound
That my belly makes, full of jelly, bouncing on the ground.
Wednesdays are my shopping days. This is my favourite time;
I love choosing all my jellies; raspberry, strawberry, orange, lime.

Fridays are my bath days but they can prove rather tricky.
The jelly party yesterday has made the bath all sticky.
I smell my fur, I smell my feet. I really need a wash.
I scrub myself with the garden broom and a bottle of orange squash.

I'm not a scary monster and I would not eat you up,
I just like eating jelly from a bowl or from a cup,
My name is Fred the Monster, so please remember me;
Every time you have a bowl of jelly for your tea.

Wendy Farley

All Because Of Me

No longer that green, clean air surrounds us.
The atmosphere is like being thrown,
Yes, into a revolting ashtray.
The wind howls angrily like an Express train.
Those filthy cars grin and pollute our streets,
Making me cough and sneeze, *Achoo!*
I can no longer breathe fresh air that was once like the smell
                                    of a sweet rose.

The ozone will be destroyed,
Yes! Because of pollution.

Piles and piles of litter disturb our once green clean streets.
Paper bags are tossed like bowling balls on the road.
Dustbins blink and open and beg, 'Put the litter in.'
I dropped a broken bottle on the street,
Never thought to put it in the bin,
I saw some of the effects of pollution.
Never thought litter would cause any harm.

But then . . . I went on holiday to the sea,
Guess what I saw?
Yes, litter and cluttered broken glass
In the once sparkling clean sea.

My eyes are a fountain,
Once the fishes used to go *splash,*
In the clean and clear sea.
Now the glass that lurks in the sea
Are razor-sharp teeth
And grip the poor fish.
So now dead fish appear
At the edge of the murky, spoilt sea.
Their skin no longer present.
But only their bones, like pearls remain.
To see such a tragic sight!
What a fright!

These fish are stone-cold stones now,
Dead in a flash, because of me!
Yes, what a fright!

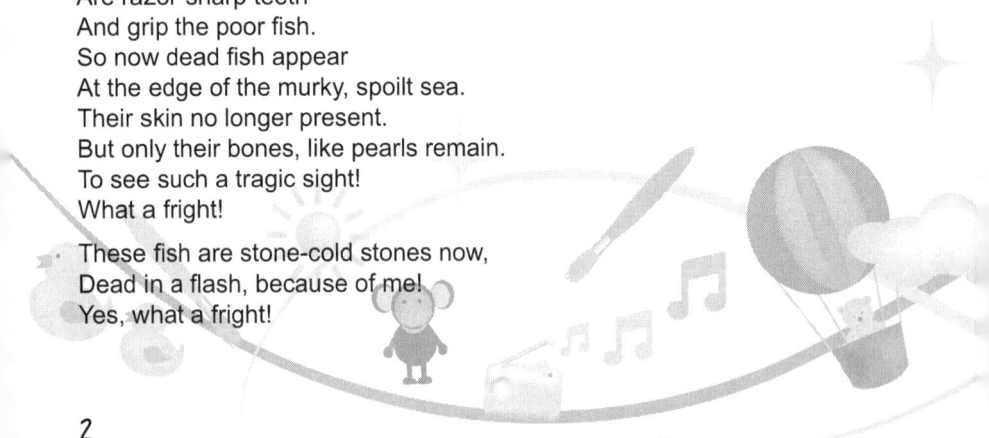

Now I must do right,
Pollution and litter are gnawing nature up,
Now I realise what I must do,
I shouldn't throw litter and pollute the Earth,
I must be responsible and recycle and be green.
'Yes, recycle the litter, recycle the bottles'
Yes, we can do this to save our nature and our Earth.

Hooray!

Afsana Taib

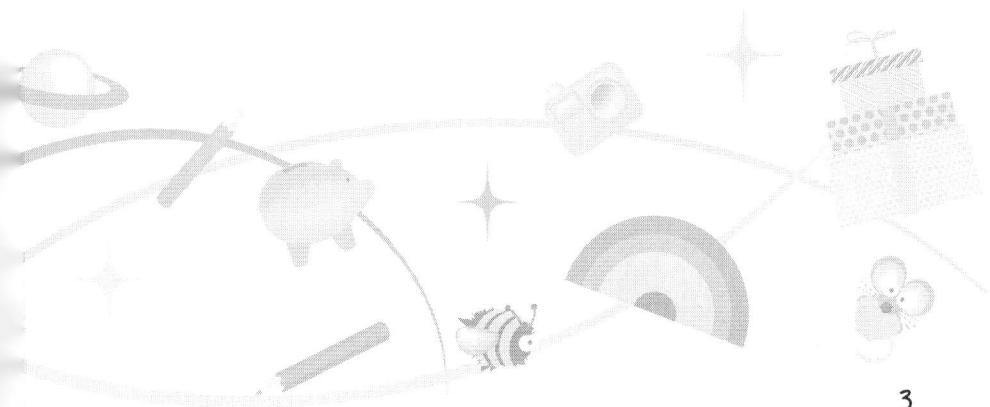

I Think My Granny Was A Witch

I think my granny was a witch,
she always wore clothes as black as pitch
Skirts that dragged upon the floor,
and a broomstick kept behind the door
Her face was pinched with a large hook nose,
she couldn't help looking like that I suppose
But I was frightened, as frightened could be,
in case she put a spell on me
She owned a cat with huge green eyes,
oh how that cat did hypnotise
So I just sat in this old brown chair,
and tried to pretend that I wasn't there
When she opened a drawer strange things fell out,
and some of them moved as they scattered about
Some had legs and an awful smell,
and her mouldy sweets made me feel unwell
Her voice was most peculiar,
like scratching nails across a jar
Piercing, screaming in my head,
oh how these visits I did dread
She hated children you could see,
especially my brother and me
An apple to us she always gave,
as she led us down to Grandad's grave
In the garden marked by a big black rod,
I always thought that a little odd
Dead people go to the cemetery,
not in the garden under a tree
'Well, eat it up,' she'd squawk in my ear,
and I would obey, transfixed with fear
Grubs and all went down my throat,
and she would stand and she would gloat
She'd lead us back up to the house,
where we would often see a mouse
Or two, or three or four, or more,
in fact they were all over the floor

I'd hold my skirt between my knees,
and close my eyes and pray, 'God please
Don't let them crawl over my toes,
and please mice, don't go up my nose'
This house had such a musty smell,
and cobwebs from the ceiling fell
Upon my face, upon my head,
the whole place filled myself with dread
And then sometimes we'd need the loo,
but had to make a bucket do
Mother always took us there,
and we would plead, 'No, it's not fair'
It never went without a hitch,
and I'm sure my granny was a witch.

Jackie Davies

Rainbow Hill

There is a little daisy out there
Whose face is yellow but petals are fair
Next to that sunflower who grows and grows
How tall? I'm not sure anyone knows
There's a rose with petals of cherry-red
Whose thorns will prick you if a bad word is said
About the flowers that live up on Rainbow Hill
With their herbaceous friends
Rosemary, Thyme and Dill
Who regularly talk with Nettle and Thistle
Who sway in the breeze as the wind does whistle
While Grass and Clover do cover the ground
The other flowers sit up high, kindly looking down
On the little bug people in the little bug mound
That sits just below Rainbow Hill's flower town.

Kim Davies

Bears

You can never be too old to have a teddy bear.
They comfort you when you're tired and sad,
Or when your mum's not there.

They come in all shapes and sizes,
In different disguises,
In any colour you want.

They can fit in pockets, sandpits,
Under covered wraps,
In buggies, prams, satchels and briefcases,
They like to take a nap.

To have one is to hold one
With bare-faced, soft, fur cheek.
To love one and to keep one,
Doesn't mean you're weak.

Nicole Touye

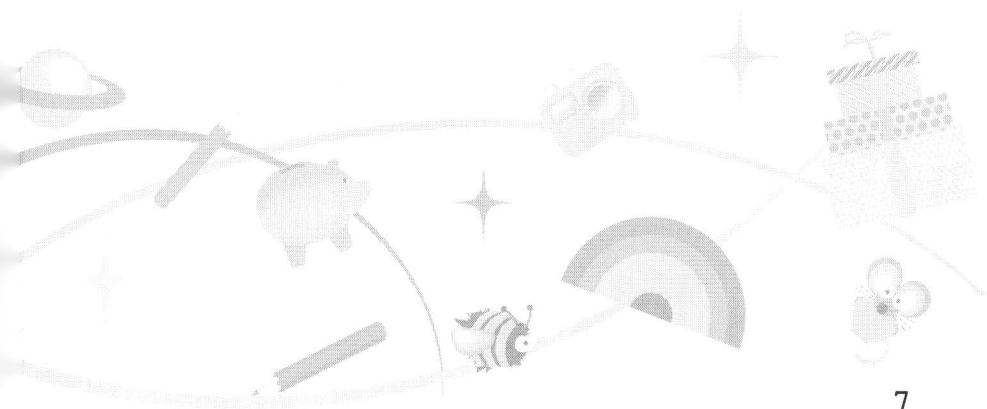

Reeds

Underneath the surface all is tension and strife
as young river horse reeds
saddle the water to take up new life.
As they break through the surface
their streaming green manes,
harden to become green armour which
protects them from the current's strain.

First of trees, a marginal guardian,
holding back the Celtic hordes
from the murky underworld of Annwn.
Yet a supple, plaited, green bed
for Moses they made,
and gave pen and paper so that
early writers could craft their trade

From the woven seat of a kitchen chair,
to the golden brown, bird-haunted
hat that chocolate box cottages wear,
by the barge load, sickle-cut and hoarded.
Yet concealed within its green-throated stem
is a constellation of spiny suns
waiting to explode with life again.

Deborah Gaudin

A Child Once More

'Come on Granny, let's hide, there's a lion at the door.'
Quickly rushed over toy-cluttered sitting room floor.
We dived through the entrance of her pink princess tent,
Inside the domed shape, several minutes we spent.

Following Granddaughter's orders, time for next game,
With little one, no two visits ever the same.
Have to forget all of my aches and feeling sore,
Revert to being a small child myself, once more.

With our shared imagination, play for hours,
Before at the end of day, she jumps in the shower.
Then it's favoured story before falling asleep,
Her mum hears nothing 'til dawn, not even a peep.

Susan Mullinger

A Song For Christmas

Why does it never snow at Christmas?
All we ever get is cloud and wind and rain.
I want a snowball fight,
And keep playing out till night,
When I get frozen to my ears and to my toes.
I want to build a snowman
That looks remotely human
With a woolly hat, and carrot for its nose.

So why does it never snow at Christmas?
All we ever get is cloud and wind and rain.

It used to snow so hard
It would cover every yard
And make people sink in deep up to their knees.
But they'd go sledging down the hill,
And get a marvellous thrill
From zooming in and out among the trees.

So why does it never snow at Christmas?
All we ever get is cloud and wind and rain.

If you look at all the cards,
When people send regards,
They all have snow scenes, every one:
With their robins and their holly
And their Father Christmas jolly
And the children having lots and lots of fun.

So why does it never snow at Christmas?
All we ever get is cloud and wind and rain.

And we're stuck indoors with family
And there's nothing on the telly
Until it's 'Harry Potter' yet again!

And we've finished all the chocolate
Which leaves us rather desolate -
Because outdoors it's cloud and wind and rain.

So why does it never snow at Christmas?
All we ever get is cloud and wind and rain.

Fran Harris

The Chef Who Couldn't Cook

Many, many years ago before you or I were born,
There lived a man who couldn't cook, not even a sweetcorn.
He tried job after job, but his meals were always burnt black
And from each and every job, he always got the sack.

Then, the luckless chef got a job in a small baker's shop.
This time he made sure his cooking was not a complete flop.
He mixed the dough using a tatty, old recipe book.
Next, he carefully put the dough in the oven to cook.

After that, he went out to lunch feeling very happy.
From the shop, he bought juice and a sandwich, which was snappy.
However, hen he returned back to the small baker's shop,
The unfortunate chef knew again, he would get the chop.

The whole of the small bakery was on fire and burning.
The fire was rapidly spreading from building to building.
Before long, the entire city of London was ablaze.
Firemen and Londoners were struggling in the scorching haze.

Who was the culprit? All the Londoners wanted to know.
To reveal the answer, they decided they would all go
To Downing Street and petition to the Prime Minister.
The Prime Minister was powerful and their new leader.

The Prime Minister admitted he hadn't a clue.
So, all the Londoners decided what they should do.
They resolved to go to the Police Inspector's top chief.
The chief could always solve any crime or catch any thief.

The top chief questioned the Londoners, one by one
To find out the place they were at, when the fire had begun.
The Londoners all said, they were at home having dinner,
The chief knew a clue must have been left by the sinner.

It was important to know, if they were telling the truth.
The chief needed to discover some reasonable proof.
He enquired, if the Londoners could accurately say,
If someone was behaving unusually that day.

A baker's shop in Pudding Lane, the Londoners did tell,
Was the first location, they discovered the burning smell.
The small baker's shop could contain the clue, the chief would need
To capture the person, who committed the dreadful deed.

He went to the shop, opened a cupboard and took a look.
Inside, the chief discovered a half-burnt recipe book.
The top chief inspector, looked inside the book in his grasp
And then, the top chief slowly released an enormous gasp.

The information the top chief had discovered was new.
The owner of book, was definitely the right clue.
For the new Prime Minster had never revealed before
The actual point of fact, that he was a chef no more.

The Prime Minister confessed, that he was not a leader
And that he was in fact, just an unlucky impostor.
He was jealous of his brother, who was a better cook.
That's why the Prime Minister gave the cooking a bad look.

The inspector and the Londoners, were very relieved.
The dreadful crime was unravelled and the culprit seized.
There was one last, big surprise for all of the Londoners.
The plague was gone and the rats were no longer commoners.

Inderjeet Deusi

I Never Liked Bananas

I never liked bananas, I never liked the feel
I never liked the way you had to pull back all the peel
I didn't like their bright yellow hue
But Grandma said, 'They're good for you.'

So now I've started to eat just one or two
But my horrible sister gobbles the last few
Now that she knows I like the taste
She says she eats them cos they might go to waste

She doesn't play the game; she doesn't play it fair
She eats the last banana before I've had my share
She does it by means quite stealthily
Because she's older and eats healthily

But I've devised a devious little plot of my own
I told her like a fat chimpanzee she had grown
And then I hid inside the peel
A slippery worm that made her squeal!

Elizabeth Ann Farrelly

I Saw

I saw a little robin
On my window sill
I tried to take a picture
But he wouldn't keep still.

I saw a little tractor
Ploughing up a field
I tried to catch him looking
At the telly's X Factor.

I saw a field of sheep
Munching up the grass
I tried to say hello
But fell right asleep.

I saw a little boat
Sailing down the river
I put on my coat
And began to shiver.

I saw a fire engine
Ringing the bell
Was it an emergency?
Who can tell?

Pauline Pickin

The Smile

When every little teardrop falls
an angel trips and sadness calls
up in Heaven way up on high
higher than the brightest sky

Cry not a tear, oh little one
there are plenty of smiles up in the sun
from up in Heaven, it's a joy to see
everyone's happy and smiles with glee

If you ever feel so sad
when times are hard and things so bad
remember God is watching you
way up in the shiny blue

So smile away each and every day
you'll help an angel on his way
dancing in the midday sun
it's time for happiness, joy and fun.

James Peace

Fairy Story

A tiny fairy, petite, sweet and small
Had nowhere to stay or go at all
So as her home she used my head
A nest made of hair she used as her bed.

People looking at me thought my hair
Was unusually kept, uniquely rare
But my head was ever kept warm
Magically dry, come rain or storm.

It's true I tell you, true, believe me
She will make you believe, as you will see
A magic spell she has cast on you
Not eight but ten toes, you have now grew.

Christopher Slater

Tall Tale

I climbed a mountain early today
took a rocket to the moon
I walked on the lunar surface
and played Quidditch with the queen
I rode a bike on a whale's back
he must have been a thousand feet long
then with one great *woooosh* of his blowhole
he sent me zooming right to Mars
I fell and tripped and fell through space
landing in a zoo
and the daddy gorilla picked me up and sat me on his knee
in his big gorilla voice, he said, 'Would you like to stay?'
I said, 'No, I can't, I've got to get home or I will be late for my tea.'
So I said goodbye to the gorilla and all his animal friends
and I borrowed enough for my bus fare home from a gang
                                              of orang-utans
the hyena gave me a ride to the station, he laughed and
                                              told me jokes
and there I was waiting for the 22 bus
the wind was blowing really hard and, cos I'm only small,
it lifted me up right to the sky and left me on a cloud
the cloud was so big and comfy that I nearly fell asleep
then with one big bang, the cloud thundered and I slid down
                                              a lightning streak.

I landed on a giant's nose but it was OK because he was asleep
and I climbed down his nasal hair, right down to his feet
I ran and ran all the way home cos I knew I was late for my tea
'And that's where I have been Mum . . . I have . . . honestly.'

My mother looked down at me and gave me a little grin
she said, 'My, oh my, my little man, haven't you had an exciting day?'
Now I'm here all tucked up in bed, ready to fall asleep
to dream of more adventures . . .
and more tall tales to tell.

Steven Corlett

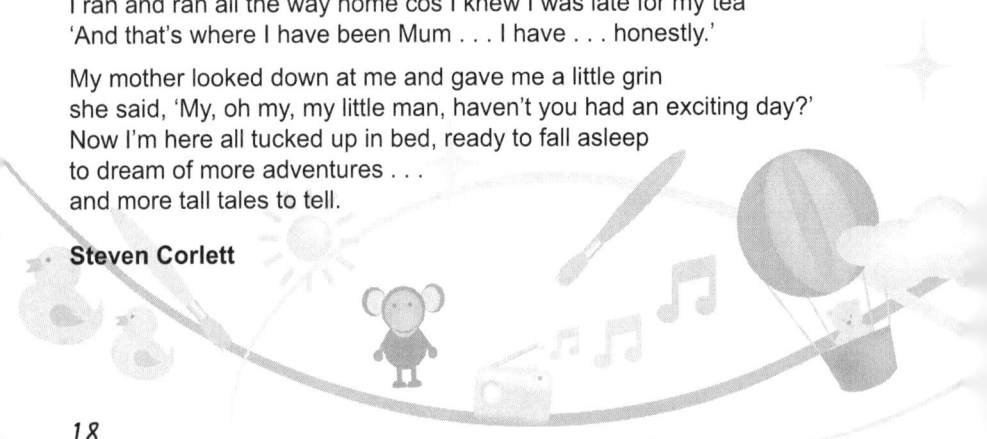

Big Boy

Please don't kiss me on the cheek
Or ruffle up my hair
Please don't cry when I'm in line
Pretend that you don't care

Don't hug or even cuddle me
Don't stroke my baby face
Don't check my socks
Don't zip me up
Or meddle with my lace

Please try to let me go to school
Like all the other boys
And try to keep your mind off me
By clearing up my toys

It won't be long before I'm home
Please try not to be sad
Just think about me playing up
Remember, when I'm bad.

Kathy Charvin

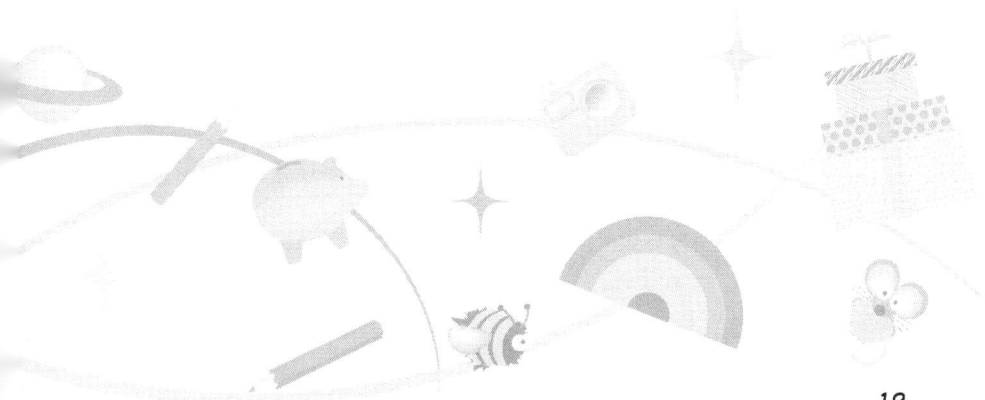

Mr Keeper Said

'Please Mr Keeper.
Can we see your zoo?
There's me and little Lilly
And our brother Josh too.'

Mr Keeper smiled,
Turned to us and said,
'I could let you see,
All my animals being fed.'

Mr Keeper said,
'Now where shall we start?
Let us find old Dobbin
And ride inside his cart.'

Mr Keeper said,
'See those old brown bears.
They spend every day,
Eating apples, plums and pears.'

Mr Keeper said,
'Can you see the llamas?
They can't eat enough,
Of buns and ripe bananas.

Mr Keeper said,
'Hear those squawking parrots?
They are searching all around
For nuts, seeds and carrots.'

Mr Keeper said,
'Can you count all the mice?
They all come from China,
And I feed them on fried rice.'

Mr Keeper said,
'Say hello to Sidney Snake.
He lives inside a snake pit,
And loves his apples baked.'

Then Mr Keeper said,
'That's the end of the zoo.
I've enjoyed all your company
And hope you have too.'

We all said, 'Yes,'
We've had a lovely day.'
And waved to Mr Keeper
Then went on our way.

Patricia Lay

I Wanna Be A Wallaby

I wanna be a wallaby
marsupials have more fun,
they live their lives
in leaps and bounds
and winter in the sun.

They always seem so happy
you never hear them grouch:
the children can stay up late -
they're never sent to bed -
instead
they're taken everywhere
with lots of bouncing fun:
they ride around
and sleep so sound
with their soft and comfy mum -
the wonders of a pouch!

Kevin Goldstein-Jackson

A Game Of Chance

Into our house, ran a white rabbit,
Jeffrey by name, how we all tried to grab it,
He ran under the table, knocked over a chair,
Jeffrey scampered to and fro, he just didn't care.

We really did chase him as fast as we could,
Jeffrey knew this, at least we thought he should,
He just scampered wherever he thought he might be safe,
Jeffrey, so wise, it surely was us that he couldn't face.

Suddenly the stairs, *oh no,* we all thought, *not the stairs,*
Jeffrey paced each step, taking them in pairs,
Away he raced, along the landing, into a bedroom,
Jeffrey knew the bed he could hide under, belonging to whom.

But not under the bed did *Jeffrey* go,
'No, no, no, under the duvet, tucked well below,
Jeffrey stayed perfectly still, as quiet as could be,
None of us thought of looking there for he.

After a while we grew tired of the search,
We guessed *Jeffrey* had used his assert,
Somehow or other we had found it quite fun,
Chasing *Jeffrey,* a *white rabbit,* an illusion, or reality,
We didn't really mind, we were just glad he'd come.

Lorna Tippett

Ants

What do people think of ants?
Just useless creatures perhaps?
But ants are tiny and especially good,
At fitting through really small gaps.

Imagine one day, you went out of your house,
Closed the door, without taking your keys.
An ant could slip through the keyhole for you,
Or the letterbox even, with ease.

Once inside though, there's one slight flaw,
It's a problem that niggles and lingers.
The ant won't be able to open your door,
As he hasn't got hands or fingers!

Kevin Landrum

Reading's Cool

I really love to read my books,
whatever they may be.
Perhaps some Harry Potter
or some lovely poetry.
I also love a mystery,
or ghost stories galore,
it doesn't matter what I read,
I always want some more!
There are fairy tales, adventures,
animals and birds,
so many lovely books to read,
so many lovely words.
People often ask me
what I'll do when I am grown.
I often say, 'One day I'll write
a story of my own.'

Jillian Henderson-Long

The Bouncy Red Ball

One day Ned was bored and feeling quite blue,
He'd played with his toys and had nothing to do.
He'd pestered his mum, who had said to him, 'Ned.
Do you think you could play somewhere else instead?
I'm busy cooking something tasty to eat
So get out of the kitchen and from under my feet.'
Ned went to the hall and, scratching his head,
Considered what toy he could play with instead,
When he suddenly spotted his bouncy red ball
Lying beside him, next to the wall.

Ned said, 'Look Mum, what I found in the hall
It's my favourite toy, my bouncy red ball.'
And before his mum could tell him to stop
He'd thrown it up high and it started to drop
It fell back down with so much force
It knocked over the saucepan and spilt all the sauce.
'The dinner is ruined,' cried Ned's mum in despair,
'And just look at this mess, there is sauce everywhere.
The kitchen is not the right place to play ball
Take it out of here now and go play in the hall.'

Ned sat at the foot of the stairs feeling glum
Twiddling the ball between fingers and thumb.
Until he thought of a game he could play with his ball
A game he could play on the stairs in the hall.
He threw his ball with all of his might
Up the ten steps to the top of the flight
It hit the wall and rebounded back,
Tumbling down and into his lap.
His next throw was a little off course
It had too much spin and much too much force.
It bounced off the wall and went here and there
It bounced off the ceiling and back down the stair.
It zoomed past Ned's ear as it flew round the hall
Knocking coats off their pegs and prints off the wall
Hearing the crash Ned's mum rushed to the door
And, surveying the mess all over the floor,
Said to her son at the foot of the stair,
'Take your ball to your room and play with it there.'

Up in his room Ned played with his ball,
Throwing it against the ceiling and wall,
It bounced on the dresser, the wardrobe and bed,
The bookshelf, the toy box and even Ned's head.
Then, all of a sudden, there was a great crash
Then a bang and a thud, a clunk and a smash.
Mum hurtled upstairs and threw open the door
And, seeing Ned's things strewn all over the floor
She said with a sigh, 'It would be better I guess
If you played in the garden once you've cleaned up this mess.'

A little while later, the mess cleared away,
Ned went into the garden and started to play.
'Now this is the right place to play ball,' said his mum
'You can throw it about and have lots of fun.
I reckon you'll be out there playing for hours
You can do what you like, but just mind my flowers.'
Sadly Ned's mum didn't foresee
The damage resulting from throw number three,
A rogue throw that bounced first left and then right
Which Ned couldn't catch, try as he might.
Things might have been better had he stopped to recall
That sometimes you must take your eye off the ball.
Instead Ned knocked over bags full of weeds,
Crashed into the bird tray and spilt all the seeds,
He chased round the fishpond and scared all the newts,
And trampled the flowers with his big, heavy boots.
And just when it seemed to be slowing down
The ball hit a spade which was stuck in the ground.
Ned tried to catch it, but it fell from his grasp
And crashed into the greenhouse and broke lots of glass.
The noise brought his mum out from indoors
Who said to her son after a very long pause,
'There are still a few hours left before it gets dark
So pick up your ball and we'll go to the park.'

Down in the park there was plenty of space
To throw and to kick and to run and to chase.
So at last Ned had found somewhere to play
With his ball and his mum for the rest of the day.

Freya Morris

There Was An Old Woman

There was an old woman of whom it's been told,
was so good at cricket, for England she bowled,
she took seven wickets, all in one day,
and would have bowled more, but bad light stopped play.

There was an old woman, while spending a penny,
fell down the toilet, not one time but many,
she thought it was funny, as she clambered back out,
clutching a wellington boot and a trout.

There was an old woman, so I've heard,
thought she could fly, the daft old bird,
she jumped off a tower, of far-reaching height,
and believe it or not, flew into the night.

There was an old woman, I don't know her name,
who built and designed, a purple steam train,
a king said, 'I'll buy it, then wanted another,
one for his wife, his mother and brother.

There was an old woman, according to many,
could dance a wild jig, on the edge of a penny,
sail round a pond, on an old five pound note,
while towing behind her a pink rowing boat.

There was an old woman, who could leap like frog,
sing like a bird and bark lie a dog,
climb up a tree, as quick as a cat,
then hang from a branch, just like a bat.

There was an old woman, of stout appearance,
who went to her baker's, he was having a clearance,
she bought all his cream cakes and jam doughnut rings,
and said, 'Nobody move until the fat lady sings.'

There was an old woman, who went down in history,
for solving the golden gate murder mystery,
she picked up the clues, that were laid on the ground,
and that's how the nasty old villain was found.

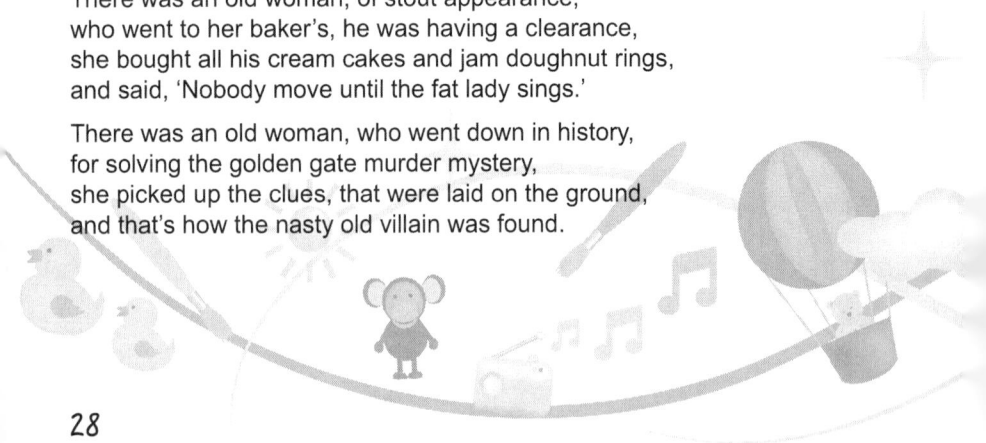

So like the old woman, who lived in a shoe,
maybe these stories, are also quite true,
or are they already, an old wives' tale?
But if they're out to amuse, they really can't fail.

Christopher Taylor

Wart

I've got a wart and it's stuck
On my hand - it's my bad luck!
I've picked it, flicked it
Filed it and gnarled it,
Rubbed it - scrubbed it!
Wished away with it -
I've even got someone to pay for it!
I've tried to freeze it,
Squeeze it
I've even tried to seize it;
But it's still there!
It's just not fair!
I've covered it and smothered it
Snipped at it - clipped at it
Hit it! Bit it!
(Although I hate to admit it)
I've pushed it, pulled it
Yanked it blanked it!
I know in time it will go away
It will disappear when I least expect one day.

Linda Lawrence

Hippo

The hippo is a friendly beast
Unless you interrupt his feast
If you do, I think you should know
He'll be angrier than if he stubbed his toe
He'll bare his teeth
And oh, good grief!
He'll bellow, shout and roar
Then, worst of all, show you the door!

Matthew Lambert

More Adventure With Santa

Santa will be arriving from a faraway land
So cold a country is jolly Lapland
I can see from a distance, he has such a lump
Putting on so much weight, he is so very plump

But there he jolly goes, riding upon his sleigh
Travelling upon the snow, on this very cold day
He jolly well makes the reindeer go even faster
Till there are a couple of jolly well disasters

Firstly, he falls off the sleigh, upon the snow
Slipping upon a slide, still singing his jolly, 'Ho, ho, ho!'
He is wriggling and mumbling, 'Ho, ho, no, no, what to do!'

The reindeers look around, their ears prop to one side
A policeman is walking towards Santa with heavy stride
He picks Santa up, giving him a ticket for jolly speeding
Santa says, 'Do you know who I am? I like to be giving

For the children,' says Santa, 'so I bid you goodnight'
The policeman says, 'I may withdraw the ticket
                                    just giving you a fright'
Off Santa goes, getting to the house, well gone 12.30
Trying to climb the chimney, but driving stuck and dirty

The chimney hasn't been swept, poor Santa gets into a muddle
Getting stuck halfway through all this jolly trouble
He manages to climb down eventually, as black as can be
Putting the children's presents on the chair, so they will see

Children, when you hear footsteps, do go back to bed and sleep
Please do not open the window to have a jolly peep
For Santa has left, he drives the reindeer through the night
So dream children, of wonderful things, till the morn brings the light

Santa is now very disguised, still jingling his bells, so full of joys
Santa goes back to jolly Laptown, after giving to little girls and boys.

Jean McGovern

In the Land Of Make-Believe

Pegasus, the last winged horse
Led the unicorns with golden horns
Through the enchanted forest
To the golden grass plains
Below the purple mountains
Where beautiful fairies played
Among exotic flowers
Chased by laughing elves with green felt hats
And no one crossed the rickety bridge
Where the troll lived far below

The moon was full and lit the way
Beneath a curtain of twinkling stars
In the land of make-believe
Where no human child ever trod
Until one bright moonlit night
When one of pure heart and soul
Entered a fairy grotto
Rode high on the back of Pegasus
Pure white-winged horse of legend
Who flew across the enchanted land
With human child of pure heart
Who chased the elves and laughed with glee
But never crossed the rickety bridge
Where the troll lived far below

Lay to rest on a feathery bed
Covered in emerald-green silk
In the enchanted land of fairies
Fell into a deep, deep sleep
Awoke in the world of un-enchantment
And hugged a cuddly teddy bear.

David M Walford

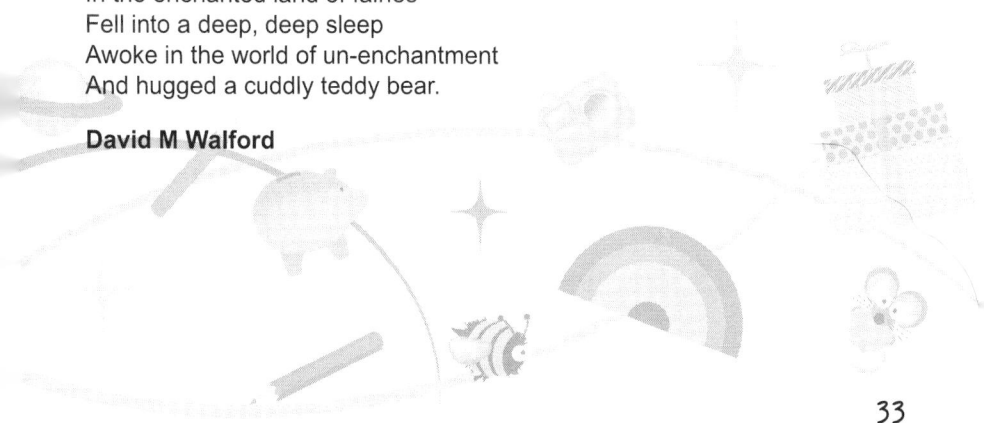

Beaches

Beaches on my holiday usually warm, white and sandy.
Hot and fine between the toes, running through my 'handy'.
'Infancy' is supposed to be very, very happy.
Not when all the 'soggy' sand is in and around your nappy.

Chafing, scratchy, uncomfortable in the extreme.
Especially when my mummy wants me to 'beam'.
Silly, frilly cap upon my head. 'I am hungry and wish to be fed.'
'I've had enough! Mum is at it again, attention-seeking all too plain.'

There is half the beach in and around my 'private parts'
Can't she find it in her heart, to rid me of this 'soggy mess'?
If she does not, I will not impress.
What I will do now, she will never guess.

Ah, that's better, what a relief.
'That soggy mess' lying at my feet.
Now my mum will have to come and wash around my 'tortured bum'!

Ellen Spiring

A Friend For Mickey

Although it was very early, all was busy on the farm,
everyone was so excited and found it hard in keeping calm.

After months and months of waiting, next door's farm had pups for
sale and the farmer's wife had chosen the one with the broken tail.

It was to be a friend for Mickey, he had heard the farmer say,
so Mickey waited by the door and wouldn't from it stray.
When the puppy came, the house was filled with all their shouts of glee and
for a moment Mickey felt left out, *nobody has noticed me!*

They laughed at everything he did, even at the puddle on the floor,
who would think a little ball of fur could cause such a big uproar!
But when the puppy spotted Mickey, he cuddled in real close,
and Mickey's heart just melted when he licked him on the nose.

They decided they would call him Jack, it wasn't hard to say,
so Mickey and Jack became the best of friends as together they would play.

Now the farmer's wife had a new straw hat and Jack could not resist
a chew, so to keep him out of trouble Mickey hid it in his bed out
of view.

Wash day came and all was revealed when the farmer's wife
cleaned out Mickey's bed, 'Oh you naughty boy, Mickey,
you can stay out of the house and sleep in the kennel instead!'

So with his head hung down and his tail tucked in, Mickey looked
a sorry sight, but when the farmer heard about the hat, he soon
had things put right.

'It's a fact of life,' he told his wife, 'all puppies like to chew, and covering up
for his little brother is what Mickey felt he must do.'

Well to make things up to Mickey, they gave him chicken for his tea
and as far as I know they are getting on fine as one happy family.

Eileen Wilbey

35

Lamenting A Clock

I'm willing to grant that while you are quite clever
To beat me repeatedly at each endeavour,
I think that it's time to say what's on my mind:
That clocks are impatient and fiercely unkind.

You hang around straight-faced all night and all day
With nothing of any great interest to say,
Except for the *tick* and occasional *tock*
Reminding me merely, that you *are* a clock!

This *ticking* and *tocking* is all very well
For keeping the time so that time, I can tell;
But this kind of 'language' can only translate
To *tisking* and *tutting* at me when I'm late!

And high on your mantle no smile, but instead -
A judgmental scorn as you near shake your head.
If only a timepiece could pardon my flaw
Without so much circling and keeping the score.

If you were a loved one you might hold my hand.
If you were an hourglass I'd give you more sand!
Musicians accommodate time with a 'pause',
A friend who's kept waiting would wait, just because.

But you have no feeling like any of these,
You just do your job without care, yet with ease.
To you, Clock, who screams every morning at me,
I wish you would *tick-tock* less adamantly!

Angela Morrison

The Fearsome Apple

There was an apple on a tree,
ripe, red and juicy,
eaten, he didn't want to be,
afraid of the big, sharp teeth
he had seen in his dreams.
The sun was smiling onto him,
his brothers laughed and played,
autumn came with hungry children,
who ate all the apples away.
Trembling with fear our apple saw
those big white teeth with awe,
'Help, help, I don't want to die!'
with great fear he cried,
but the teeth only tickled him,
so he started laughing
and laughed more and more
as he slid down a boy's throat.
'Hui, that's fun!' he said,
getting thinner and thinner again,
Swimming in the deep stomach sea;
what was left of him finally,
were pure healthy vitamins
travelling through the boy's veins,
who said, 'Thank you! You gave me life,
my hunger is now satisfied!'
Our brave apple was proud
of the job he had done
and laughed about his fear so loud,
the boy thought he heard his tummy rumble.

Sydney Krivenko

Rumble Tum

Do you know my good friend Rumble Tum?
He lives around the corner near me and my mum
When we go to the park with our little dog Bob
He often is working, just doing his job.

He watches each day in his own special way
The golden brown leaves as they dance and they play.
At night he allows them to fall, sweep and glide
But each autumn morning, they're brushed to one side.

The berries are russet and crimson, bright red
It's Rumble's first job as he gets out of bed
The brown ones are sorted and soon disappear
The shiny new bright ones glow through to New Year.

Pine cones are waiting for children at play
Collecting those fallen for school the next day,
As each one is ripened it's touched by his hand
There are some here for everyone just as he planned.

He waits and he waits for the best time of all
As autumn fades out and the winter months call
The chill of the air, the quick changing light
The white glistening frost and the sharpness of night.

It's Christmas at last and with all his work done
My Rumble Tum rests and begins to have fun
Ready for a holiday this time of year
And like all the rest of us full of good cheer.

His job is all done until Spring nods her head
But until that time he'll stay tucked up in bed
Then snowdrops will tap on his window once more
He'll be ready for action and run out through his door.

A sprinkling of yellow for daffy down dillies
A puff of sweet scent for the newly born lilies
The stripes not quite ready for bees in their hive
But golden dip offered as blackbirds arrive.

His message to you and to all children near
Is look all around you and don't be in fear
Of trees, flowers, creatures, all that you see
Treat them kindly, respect them and let them be free.

Shelley Fairclough

A Very Hungry Caterpillar

(Inspired by 'The Very Hungry Caterpillar' by Eric Carle)

A very hungry caterpillar
Went crawling in the sun.
His stomach started to grumble,
So he ate an apple - one.

Still hungry was the caterpillar
He wasn't sure what to do.
So he went in search of juicy pears,
And munched his way through two.

On Wednesday he devoured plums
But his stomach was not merry.
Found a patch of red delights,
And ate four big strawberries.

Five oranges down, so juicy sweet
Was Friday's meal for him.
But Saturday he ate some treats,
That did not keep him thin.

On Sunday his poor stomach ached
Full of all that food.
He ate a leaf so big and green,
That made him feel quite good.

Now Caterpillar was not so small,
And his appetite was now gone.
He worked upon another task
And built himself a home.

For two long weeks he stayed inside
Confined in his cocoon.
At last he nibbled his way out,
And emerged out of his room.

What a surprise for this insect
As he flew into the sky.
He'd changed inside his little home,
And was now a butterfly!

With two wings full of colour,
And antennae too like prongs.
Our very hungry caterpillar
Flew away, good luck, so long!

Helen Moll

Twinkle

Come, gather up the stardust,
Enrol for singing, drama, dance.
Early learning, your teddy will enhance.
Bring him to dance with you.
Pre-school dance, we'll see you through
When you perform you solo tu-tu.

Betty Bukall

The Planet Boo

The planet Boo is a funny place,
Full of a very peculiar race,
'Gumbles' is their name,
Rather silly but tame,
They don't run fast or walk slow but have a strange pace.

Boo is a very bright and colourful land,
Where all the ground is made from sand,
There is red, pink and blue,
Green and yellow on Boo,
They even have their own musical band.

They don't have food as such,
Rather flavours that they just touch,
Peanut butter and jellies,
Seem to fill their bellies,
They're so small they don't need much.

If you ever have the chance, then visit Boo,
You will really love it, I promise you,
From the musical band,
To the colourful land,
Go on, pay it a visit, you know you want to.

Marie Date

Gadgets Galore!

You don't need the latest gadget,
What you have is better by far,
You carry it with you wherever you go
You can play it wherever you are

Just use your imagination,
Let the adventure commence,
Go in search of your destiny,
Lose yourself in the suspense.

You'll find dragons, brave knights in their castles,
Huge giants or fairies so small.
However often you play the game
Each time it's sure to enthral.

Everyone's game will be different,
Each one will be unique,
Living your own adventure,
Creating your own mystique.

You need no television,
No computer nor console; instead,
The only screen you can play it on
Is the screen that is inside your head!

Kath Cooley

Silly Billy

Billy was a joker,
Who made the neighbours mad.
One day he overstepped the mark,
Got wrong side of his dad.
Now Billy's not so silly,
Anymore.

Paul Kelly

Transformers

They tuck into their food
with great gusto;
munching steadily in neat rows
and stripping plants bare.
Such good nourishment
means they grow rapidly,
shedding their skins several times
as they become too small for their bodies.
When the time is right,
they lock themselves away
in a protective case,
emerging in due course
as nectar-loving creatures -
magnificent moths or beautiful butterflies.

Annabelle Tipper

The Adventures Of Bevon

There was an old dog called Bevon,
Next birthday he'd be eleven.
He could not wait,
For a big chocolate cake,
So he wanted to travel to Devon.

Bevon, he needed to drive,
But he crashed into a beehive.
The bees they swarmed down,
Pinning him to the ground,
It's a wonder he's still alive.

A farmer was passing that way,
On a shimmering, bright summer's day.
He picked Bevon up,
Threw him into his truck,
Next to the bales of hay.

Bevon, he tried to wake up,
But his eyes were covered in muck.
'Don't worry lad,
It can't be that bad.
It's time you 'ad some good luck.'

His rumbling stomach concaved,
So he told the thing to behave.
Lying there on the seat,
Was a package so neat,
Of the chocolate cake that he craved.

Amber Roskilly & Clare Roskilly

Children On A Christmas Morn

Children are out into the street,
Almost barren, there dense
Fog settles on everything -
Towers, domes, church steeples,
Defying the happy Xmas morn;
Children are rushing, joying and dancing,
As if, from the very womb of Earth;
Unhappily they seem thrown into
A sullen world of woe;
Knowing not what distress awaiting;
Yet, they seem happy with the thought
It's the holy Christmas morn
Their spirits so moved with
The Holy Father, sweet divine,
They would ever be filled with
Adoration deep and love so earnest,
In sheer expectation of a holier rebirth!
Fog soon melts into a gleaming
Sphere of golden beauties,
The sun pours out all the soft
Molten beams instinct with life and beauty,
The world itself turns into a new Heaven
Preparing for rebirth of all!
Twittering birds round and round
The turrets and chapels feel such
Impulses sweetening all about!

Prof Kalyan Ray

My Doggy

Your hair's all wrong.
You bark too long.
You poo and wee
Then sit on me.
You rub your nose
On my new clothes
And lick my food -
Mum thinks you're rude.
She thinks you smell
And come from Hell,
And likes you less
When there's a mess.
But I forgive
Your canine ways.
My doggy, these
Are happy days.

Joe Hoyle

Three

I'm thinkin' 'bout Winken, and Blinken and Nod,
And Hickory, Dickory, Doc:
Three sail off in a wooden shoe,
And three hang out in a clock!
Now would you try shoeing instead of canoeing
Or hang with a *tick* and a *tock*?

It's three little kittens that lost all their mittens
And haven't a clue where they're at.
A mother confronted with this lapse of mind
Must be one dispirited cat.
I'm telling you love, when I lose a glove,
I hear for a year about that.

And speaking of animals, and about three,
Remember those blundering bears
Who leave for a short little stroll in the woods
And are taken for all of their wares
By one little blonde who is overly fond
Of porridge and bedding and chairs?

Or three little mice that run riot 'round farms.
(It's a sad tale because they are blind.)
But shouldn't mice try to avoid farmers' wives?
At least farmers' wives who aren't kind?
To tempt farmers' wives who are brandishing knives
Strikes me as quite weak of mind.

And one other story that's often been told:
The story of 'Three Little Pigs'.
What could be as silly as houses of straw
Or houses of nothing but twigs?
A wolf on attack wouldn't need half a pack
To out-distance these loose whirligigs.

Now I've heard of three wise men, and three sailing ships

That Columbus took far out to sea,
And also three witches who torment Macbeth;
These threesomes don't compensate me.
Three ghosts who haunt Scrooges are balanced by stooges.
Could this be an odd number? Three!

W Penn

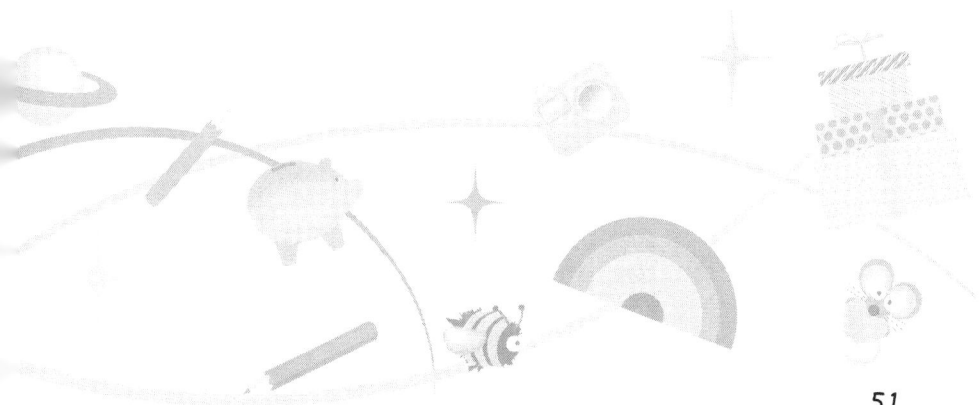

Remembering Mr MacAdam

On the motorway I saw
An upturned cone
Red like a poppy
Growing out of the tarmac

Mr MacAdam would have been proud
To see his creation
Mile on mile
Along which cars and lorries pile

Runways too are made of this
And planes take off with barely a hiss!
Remember him, we surely will
As hole and crevice with tarmac fill

Mr Hooley invented the stuff
And Mr MacAdam's road surface is tough!

Barbara Tozer

Wrong Noises

Don't miaow at that pig
A cat makes that sound
A piggy says oink
With its nose to the ground

Nor does that horse bark
That's a doggy of course
Try to say 'neigh'
That's more like a horse

Oh! Silly Billy
What are you doing now?
A sheep doesn't moo
That's the sound of a cow

And that lion won't cluck
Of that I'm sure
It's hens that cluck
A lion goes *roar!*

What's that? A worm?
It says nothing at all
Just slithers about
All slimy and small

You hissed at that snake!
What a clever young lad
Now you're just being silly
Don't snore at your dad.

Dan McPheat

Little Dora Dormouse

Little Dora Dormouse lives in the base of a tree,
She has a cosy little home, as neat as it can be.
She has her own little bed
Made up of leaves and soft, downy moss,
And a storage place for gathered food, for sunny seasons,
Through to frost.
There are intertwining passageways which lead to her front door,
And a scattering of assorted leaves to resemble a makeshift floor.
Tiny pink and purple wildflowers grow outside around the tree,
Making Dora's little home look as picturesque as can be.

Mary Plumb

On Watch

The sparkling clear glass bowl stands
On the table full of water
Inside the bowl are three goldfish
They swim ceaselessly in circles
When all is quiet someone comes.
The household cat is there to watch
He sits and watches every movement
What is he thinking about now?
Perhaps - *I'll jump on the table*
I can scoop them out with my paw
And then I'll have them for my tea
Or perhaps he's just thinking
How I wish I could swim like that!

Terry Daley

A Buck And Doe

Living in a field of lettuce was a lonely buck rabbit
Each day he would go out to eat as was his habit
He was looking for a mate to share his lettuce and home
One summer's day he decided he would go for a roam
He found another field full of juicy carrots galore
Enjoying his change of diet next day he went back for more
There sitting in the field a lady rabbit was eating
Nibbling away at the carrots, this was a chance meeting
Hopping up to her, they ate, played and had lots of fun
When it was time to part the lady rabbit was looking glum
The lady rabbit said she was lost and all alone
The buck said, 'Come back with me and share my field and home'
They now live together and the buck has lost his old habits
Stays home most nights to help to look after the baby rabbits.

Leonard A G Butler

Farmland Friends

Where the soft winds drift and blow,
There our whim of joy will go.
Be it on those sands of time,
Or that ache when love-knots twine.
So high above in mid-summer weather,
Swifts depart then fly together,
July has flown, alas, and so have they,
To return before our farmer ricks his hay.
A dairymaid sit-a triple-legged stool,
Milking cows when yield is full.
Acres across for much to graze,
Curd of milk without its whey,
Provides hard cheese at noon of play.
Coloured red and sky ablaze,
Trellised fences then paths of craze.
The shadows tint the chestnut tree,
And branches make a canopy.
Mister Mole with paws like hands,
Burrows deep in many lands,
Living inside the bark of a tree
Are beetles and wasps that we seldom see.
They all are industrious and manufacture things
From beeswax and those nasty, horrid stings.

Tom Cabin

Ode To A Footballer

My name is Jack
I play footie out the back
Or anywhere that I can kick a ball
Just to show that I'm no fool
I scored a hat trick while at school
And another in the Sunday morning game
When I grow up
I'll help Arsenal win the cup
Then everyone around will know my name
My family will be proud
And they can shout aloud
'He's our boy
And his name is Jack!'

Daphne Fryer

The Tale Of May

'Come now,' said the dog
wagging his tail
'It's the first day of May, don't you know
there's nothing better
to welcome the spring
than a heavenly roll in the snow?'

The puss tossed her head
and spat on the ground
'You try if you dare, you big clown
these are my weapons
and I'll polish your frown
if you don't immediately,
and at once, put me down'

The dog started laughing
and rolled on his back
'You are a right one, oh my dear
the only thing that you like to do
is sit by the hearth in a chair'

Puss tossed her head back
and stiffened her claws
this joke from the dog left her cold
she sneezed as she daintily
gobbled a mouse
who came in just a little too close.

Lila Joseph

A Tear To A Cloud

Attach a tear to a cloud
And let the breeze carry it away
Children you have been very sound
And the wind is whispering his way

Attach a tear to a cloud
I will gather it at dawn
Tears will fall with no sound
And the rain will be my own

The wind doesn't dare speak to me of you
He just know verses without joy
He curls up in the hollow of my hand
To hide himself until tomorrow for you

In an arid desert, the rose will blossom
If it is only a mirage
The rose is so beautiful
That I will believe it is awesome

Children go, attach a tear to a cloud
With the innocence of your hearts.
The Lord will bless all the tears
Falling on Earth from the clouds.

Victorine Lejeune Stubbs

A Star Just For You

When you climb into bed
When the day's at an end.
When you look out your window
Just dream or pretend.
See all the bright stars
Twinkle and shine.
Guess which is yours
Then guess which is mine.
For each little star
Is especially there
To watch over children.
To love them with care.
As you look up and wonder
Which star has your name
Emily or Henry
Vicky or James
There is always a bright star
That winks back at you.
Answers all your dreams.
Grants wishes, one - two.
And as your eyes close
And you fall fast asleep
A bright little star
Your safety will keep.
And when you're in dreamland
As you sleep through the night.
Your bright star beside you
Until morning light.

Joy Grant

Springhill

There is a place that's way up high,
A haven net from home,
With sunlight streaks that look like stars,
Roaring fires and brimming laughs,
And trees wherever you roam.

Magic echoes through the site,
Breathes thrills and spills and fun,
You join this close family tree,
With room for everyone.

There's a quiet understanding here,
With a patient guarding eye,
Especially as dark descends,
And the moon lights up the sky.
And when the scarlet sunset comes,
Trekking through the trees,
Renewed hope and strength and warmth appears,
Rustling across the leaves.

The heavens nurtured this place,
And set it on a hill,
To watch over its crew,
(Campers both old and new)
And affectionately named it *Springhill*

Denise Delaney

Broccoli

Who loves broccoli?
It's green and kind of knobbly.
And when my granny cooks it,
The stems are soft and wobbly.

Of course, I know it's good for me.
These green things often are.
I just wish someone would invent,
A bright green chocolate bar!

Jackie Buckle

Two Of A Kind

Oranges and lemons,
Fish and chips,
Bangers and mash,
Food to nourish
And please our taste buds.

Choose your dish,
It could be fish.

Food is so fab
For a growing lad.

Take a toasted bite
Or something light.

Aromas add pleasure
To eat at leisure.

What's for lunch?
Something to munch
And energise.
Tasty bites
And soothing soups,
Salads and chips,
Pudding and pies,
Fruit slices with ices,
All flavours and spices!

Margaret Ann Wheatley

David And Goliath

David, a shepherd, builder and musician
An outlaw, a friend, with an outgoing mission
Appeared so often in many a role
Political and military, the Israelite's soul.

David, when young, he tended his sheep
The youngest of eight, a good life he did keep
Handsome and rugged and a little roughshod
Anointed by Samuel, a warrior of God.

Boasted he'd killed a lion, and a bear
His trust in God it was always there
He volunteered to fight the Philistine giant
Refusing the armour and sword of the client.

The Philistine champion, Goliath his name
Over nine feet high, and known for his fame
Unbeaten he stood in the valley below
David with sling killed him with one blow.

The stone embedded itself in his head
This huge giant of a man now he lay dead
The spirit of the Lord had come upon him
And a hope for the future as a would-be made king.

Catherine M Armstrong

Mummy, Where's Teddy?

The garage is full right up to the roof
With boxes of all sizes and shape
Full of household items each packed with care
And sealed securely with brown Sellotope

All carefully labelled so we'll know what is where
And I am now satisfied that we're ready
I look around at my work with contentment
Then hear a scream, 'Mummy, where is my teddy?'

Floods of tears, and then screams and shouts
As my darling daughter searches each room
Behind the sofa and under the stairs
In case he is hiding there in the gloom

We all join the search just to double-check
Where she has vainly searched already
The removal men will just have to wait
For we know she won't leave without Teddy

But of her teddy there is just no sign
So in frustration and angry despair
We start to unpack all the boxes
To see if Teddy is hiding in there

But just as the last box is unpacked
We hear her call out, 'Oh, it's so funny!'
He was in the garden all of the time
'Come on let's show him the new house now, Mummy!'

Don Woods

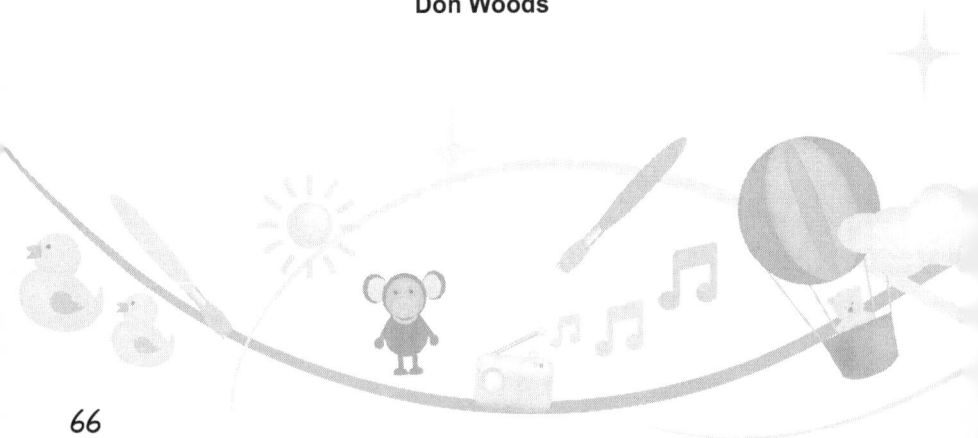

Tortoise Called Fred

When our children were young they had a tortoise called Fred
The bedding was 'The Sunday Times' and 'Express', he was
well-read
They all loved Fred, they did look after and feed him so well
When Fred heard their voices, his head would emerge from his shell

Then one day they asked us could they take him for a little stroll
All that Fred could do was slightly sway and roll
Old Fred was the most handsome tortoise, he was treated like a king
They would talk to him, he loved to hear their childish voices sing.

When the winter arrived, old friend, the tortoise, would be warm
in straw-like bed.
When the awakening time arrived, old Fred would like to be fed.
They gave Fred the best lettuces and cabbages, they must be
fresh and the best
He would have the sweetest leaves and the family would have
the rest.

When they let Fred in the garden upon fine summer's warm day
Then we searched favourite places, somebody had stolen
and taken him away.
The children were upset, he had to console them when they cried
Then we told them that Fred was old, then we said he must
have suddenly died.

When the children were young we had a tortoise named Fred.
He was the prince among tortoises, he was a gentleman,
he was well bred.
Then he offered to buy another one, they said no one could
replace our Fred
Then in the garden they lit a bonfire where they burned his bed.

J F Grainger

The Giggle Fart

Scrikklebackdondo
On the planet of Quill
Is a colourful place
Where no one gets ill.
There's also no wars
No ASBOs or drugs
The Quillans use giggling
To fight off their bugs.
If they feel a bit low
Or under the weather
Splagwoptwit appears
With his magical feather.
He'll tell a good joke
Then tickle their tums
Until giggling is heard
Coming out of their bums.

Harriet Angell

Chief Inspector Mulligan

Chief Inspector Mulligan
Was flying off to Crete,
Swapping London drizzle for
Some continental heat.

He'd packed his suitcase carefully,
His helmet and his truncheon,
And sandwiches (in case the flight
Did not provide a luncheon.)

His boxer shorts and swimming trunks
Complete with little crest,
And Eau-de-Interpol aftershave -
The girls would be impressed.

His size twelve boots were polished bright,
His efforts had been ceaseless,
His shiny-buttoned uniform
Was folded flat and creaseless.

And now he strained and heaved and puffed
To get the suitcase flattened
Down enough to ensure that
The hatches could be battened.

Eventually the catches clicked
And in their locks reposed
'Aha!' cried he, quite breathlessly
'At last, the case is closed.'

Peter Goulding

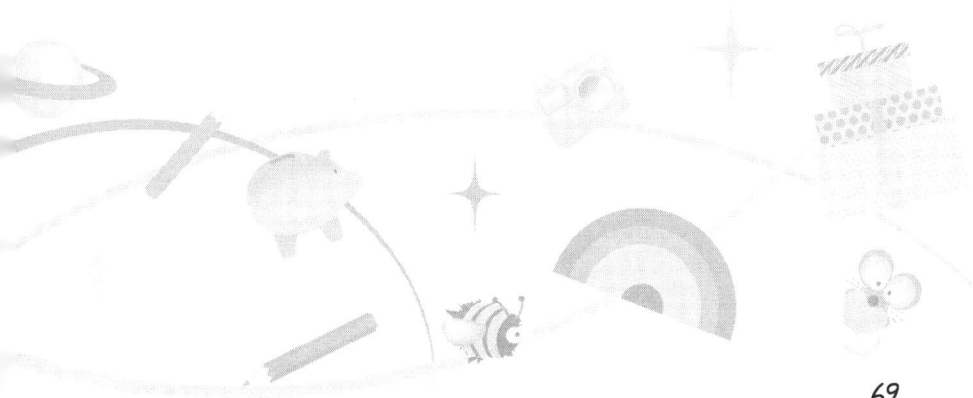

See Henry Run!

Henry won't scrub,
Henry won't rub,
Henry won't wash in his nice big bathtub!

The bathroom is free,
the sink stands in wait,
but Henry prefers his mucky old state.

Soil in his hair,
he hasn't care,
if his grubby young face makes his classmates all stare!

No flannel,
no soap,
no bubbles that float,
he's not one for water unless there's a boat!

There's a smell,
and a hum
that could make your nose numb.
but mention a wash and you'll see Henry run!

Penny Turner

Threadbare Fred Bear

My furry friend is called Fred
He sits at the end of my bed
He only has one tatty ear
Which makes it very hard to hear

Buttons for eyes in his old head
A nose stitched on, with black thread
With age his body is limp and baggy
His tummy skin now very saggy

He watches me as my life goes on
He's been around for so long
From me being a baby, tot to teen
Everything he's heard and seen

Fred saw my first steps after I crawled
Heard me chuckle and when I bawled
Shared my secrets and my fears
And when I laughed myself to tears

Fred's been there through thick and thin
Now it's time for me to care for him
I'll plump his stuffing, mend and repair
So he's no longer . . . so threadbare!

As good as new he sits on my bed
A shiny new ribbon has my Fred
He'll still watch over me, year after year
And will listen . . . with his brand new ear!

Trish Campbell

Spiders In The Zoo

A fish, they say, can swim for miles,
A shark, a whale, an elephant too,
But still I wonder all the while,
Why keep arachnids in the zoo?

There are kangaroos from far away
And wildcats from quite near,
Lions, wolves and tigers play,
But it's spiders that I fear.

Slimy, scaly snakes that hiss
And crocodiles that snap,
But I can't get my head around
Eight-leggers, what of that?

They crawl and creep into my eyes,
Up and down the glass,
A little voice inside then cries
'I'd burn em' all to ash!'

That may not be very nice to hear,
I'm not a violent child.
But I often think how best to spear,
A spider on the side.

Gorillas beat their hairy chests
And parrots squawk and laugh at you.
I'm not sure which animal I like best,
But why keep spiders in the zoo?

Sloths, baboons and otters play,
Smile and shriek and sing,
And mothers always sigh and say,
'Of course you can't go in!'

The zebras jump and laugh to think
Of lions all locked away.
Cheetahs, leopards, hyenas too,
No zebracide today!

All is well and all is good
And wonderful no doubt,
But as soon as we reach the arachnid house
I'm in and then I'm out.

There are many things I understand
Of science, maths and English too,
But please can someone tell me why,
They keep spiders in the zoo?

Adrian Scarlett

The Pudding Inspectors

The pudding inspectors
The pudding inspectors
They knock on your door
And lay down the law.

They rifle through your trifle
Check your custard
Cuts the mustard.
I've even seen them
Count the sprinkles
Sitting on the cream.

The pudding inspectors
The pudding inspectors
They burst into room
Armed with their spoons.

How airy are your fairy cakes?
Would they go down well
With Tinkerbell?
They tape the squelch
That jelly makes
And send it to the lab.

The pudding inspectors
The pudding inspectors
Should all be put on trial.
There's already a measure
For our puddingy pleasure
It's simple
It's a smile.

Duncan Jones

Untitled

A s the sun shines the storm ends.
B less this world, my family and friends.
C arry me at the crossroads
D ig a path for my life's railroads.
E very day brings something new
F orever promises we receive from You.
G od is always there,
H ere and everywhere.
I magine a world with more peace and justice
J oy and love spread across the atlas.
K ingdoms unite
L ove shining bright.
M ay the world become a better place
N ations filled with warmth on their face.
O pen hearts to release
P eace.
Q ueens and kings shall no more
R ule in tyranny and war.
S oldiers will cease
T o please
U ndivided unison.
V ictory
W ith pouring
'X citement and glory
Y ears will be shed in endless
Z ealousness.

Yolanda Mabuto

Animal Magic
(Inspired by Beatrix Potter)

Sitting by the water
I slowly close my eyes,
then hearing someone near me
I wake to a surprise.

For standing there beside me
dressed from head to feet,
is the largest Mister Rabbit
you could ever wish to meet.

He says, 'Are you alright my dear,
perhaps you've lost your way?'
and he offers me a carrot
as we pass the time of day.

I know I must be dreaming,
or my mind has finally gone,
I'm speaking with a rabbit so
I know that something's wrong.

He says, 'I must be leaving,'
and he hopes I didn't mind,
so I thank him for his trouble
and said he'd been quite kind.

I feel a bit like Alice
but this rabbit has no watch,
and continuing my journey
I then meet Mister Fox.

He is standing with a paper
the Woodland News I think,
the story of a chicken raid
is causing quite a stink.

I said I saw him sleeping
in my garden yesterday,
'A heavy night,' he winks and says,
'A vixen came to play.'

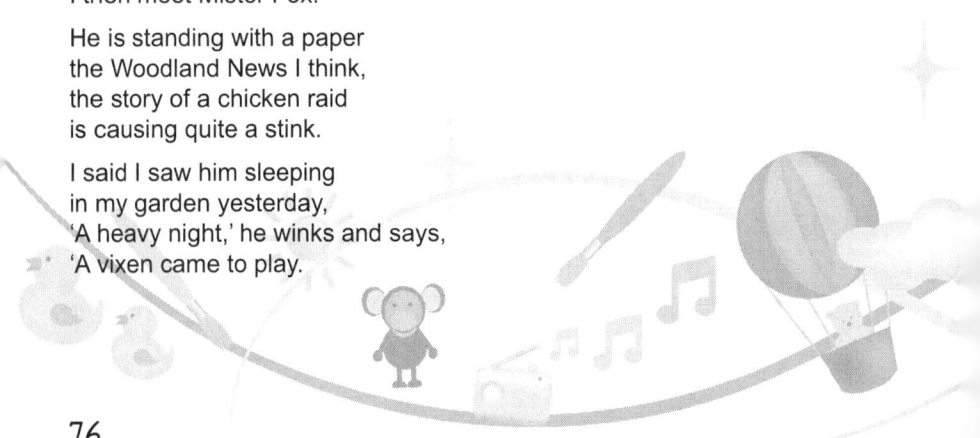

I took her out for dinner
with a touch of exercise,
there was a chicken on the menu
it was really quite a prize.'

He smiles at me and winks again
with mischief on his face,
so I said, 'I best be going,'
and then quicken up my pace.

Continuing my journey
not caring where I walk,
seeing Badger and the Porker twins
who don't have time to talk.

Then onward to the village green
where I slowly realise,
I'm turning into one of them
right before my eyes!

I'm covered now with feathers
a duck so it would seem,
I turned to run in panic
and let out a piercing scream!

Waking up, I'm only dreaming,
and said, 'Thank God for that!'
then turned and saw my father
shake hands with Mister Rat.

   Argh!

Brian Russell

The Hairy Backpacker

The hairy backpacker backpacked his way through Cairo.
There he found old lump-backed, long-legged horses,
And fellows speaking in gibberish Egyptian lingo.

The hairy backpacker discovered a water pool called the River Nile.
In pyramids and caves he saw paintings of cats,
As well as a woman named Cleopatra who didn't smile.

The hairy backpacker ended up with desert sand in his eyes.
His back hair became smelly and sweaty from being in the sun,
It was so bad he started accumulating pet flies.

The hairy backpacker packed his backpack to go home.
He had longed for a warm bubble bath, his rubber duck,
To brush his teeth and to straighten his back hair with a comb.

Samantha Carroll

Jumping Round The Garden

Jumping round the garden like a kangaroo
Bouncing up and down is so much fun to do
Why not come and join me
Then you can do it too?
You can jump around the garden like a kangaroo

Buzzing round the garden like a bumblebee
Here, there and everywhere
you won't catch me
In and out the flower beds playing happily
As we buzz around the garden like a bumblebee

Marching round the garden as tall as a giraffe
Didn't we all look silly?
Look at Mummy laugh
Daddy came and joined in and said we all looked daft
As we marched around the garden as tall as a giraffe

Tiptoe round the garden as quiet as a mouse
Trying not to make a sound
We might disturb the house
First we find a place to hide
Then seek each other out
As we tiptoe round the garden as quiet as a mouse

Lounging in the garden like a chimpanzee
Eating fresh bananas and hanging from the trees
Mummy says it's time for us to have our tea
Time to say goodnight to the lazy chimpanzee

Be sure whilst you are sleeping
The animals all are too
All of them, except of course
That naughty kangaroo.

Miacarla Britain

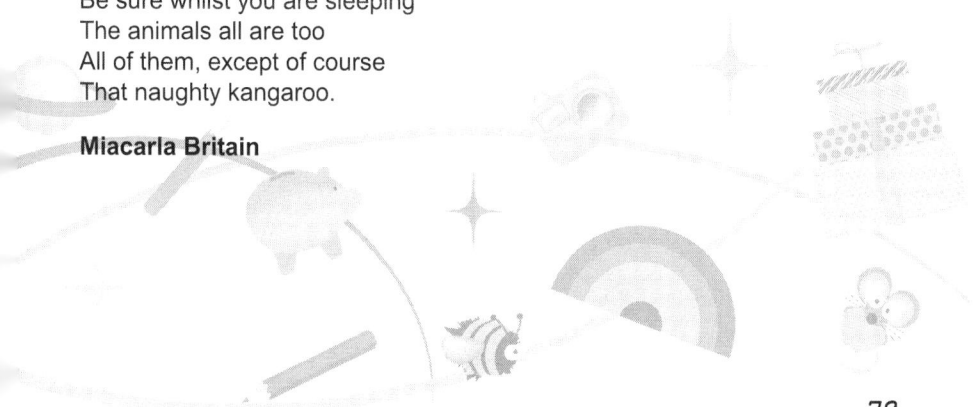

The Tale Of The Hamster Gangsters And The Criminal Cats

Once in the land of King Chip the Tenth, whose reign lasted
a very great length.
Came four robber animals, not too small, who said they were giants
but not very tall.
The chipmunks of Ham stopped to stare, and asked them
why they'd journeyed there.
But the gang was quiet and stern in mood and their leader looked
like Robin Hood.

First was Buttons, 'The Not Very Bright'. he planned all the crimes,
in the dark of night.
Long Fur Frank had the lookout's part, while Four Paws Fred,
pushed the getaway cart.
Long Tail Tom was good at disguise, he was kind to his mum
and never told lies.
The gang made a plan; to rob all the banks, steal all the acorns
and never stay thanks.

For acorns were used, like money you see, which they meant to steal
soon after tea.
But guarding the banks in the Treasury Tower, was a mean old cat,
Rowan Ben Glower.
He'd a one-eyed crony with only five lives and two ginger toms
with claws like knives.

But Buttons would not be beaten by cats and called for help
from the Yellow-belly bats.
Flying so high by the light of the stars they scared off the cats
who fled behind bars.
The gang filled a cart with acorn nuts and took home the loot
to share out the cuts.

They gave to the poor of the city of Ham and some to the bats
who helped with the plan.
Some went to save endangered fleas, some to the chipmunks
to buy more trees.
The gang escaped down Weasel Lane, and were last seen heading
for the bars of Spain.

Francis Mcdermott

Mirage

Tomorrow I will come but cannot stay
You see I borrow the time I come here
I will look through your world
Find some happiness and achieve my goal
Always stand before or behind you
We have only a chosen few.

Did you see God just pass you in the breeze?
Even in the powerful wave of the blessed sea
I will be in your dreams at night
You will feel My presence in sight
I will return to My world
A place of peace we all hold.

You see I borrow the time I come here -

If your time was short here,
What would you do before you go?

Shairoon Mohammed Sookdeo

The Newts' Sports Day

'Are you up Neville? Wake up!'
He heard his mother say
'Get out of bed and put on your kit
It's the annual Newts' Sports Day'

Neville did not need reminding
As he hated swimming races
He was the slowest newt around
He had better pack his cases

Too late! His mother was on the stairs
She would not let him go
'I know you hate the swimming races
But surely you can row

Your father was club captain
He always won the rowing
I know you've always been quite small
But lately you've been growing.'

Neville knew he was small
And the slowest in his class
He didn't want to join in the races
And hated coming last

The whistle went for the first race
Neville started his front crawl
He was still splashing, the others finished
He had never felt so small

The next race was the rowing
He got slowly in his boat
Whatever else would happen
At least the boat would float!

He heard the starting whistle blow
With all his might he started to row
His mother crying, 'Go, go, go!
I told you you're no longer slow!'

In a haze Neville passed the line
He heard his father, 'Well done son
I am so proud you did just fine
Do you believe you actually won?'

Neville couldn't believe it
His friends held him up high
But the moral of the story,
Don't give up and always try.

Louise Foster

My Sister Is An Alien

(For Jacqueline)

My sister is an alien
I've known it since her birth.
She's always acted rather strange
She's not from planet Earth

She's there when I am sent to bed.
She's there when I get up.
But her bed is never slept in.
I know there's something up.

My sister is an alien
She flies off to the stars.
Each night she's in her spaceship
Travelling to Mars.

Because she's there each morning
And we've never seen her go,
Mum never knows she's missing.
But Ted and I both know.

We thought we heard a spaceship
Outside her bedroom door.
And early the next morning
There was space dust on the floor!

My sister is an alien
I know you think she's not
But - she drinks her water with a knife
And eats her ice cream *hot*.

One day I'll catch my sister out.
I'll watch her through the night
And see her in her spaceship
Flying out of sight.

Doreen Davis

The Skiver

'Mum, I'm feeling rather funny
I feel strange inside my head
My nose is very runny
I'd better stay in bed.'

Now don't come that with me son
You're up to your old trick
Get up and get your clothes on
I don't believe you're sick.'

'But Mum, I'm feeling sort of queasy
I've got a buzzing in my ear
I'd better take it easy
I'd better stay just here.'

'Last night you seemed quite able
You were at your very best
Now breakfast's on the table
So hurry and get dressed.'

'Mum, my tummy's really aching
I've had a funny turn
You can't believe I'm faking
I'm far too ill to learn.'

'Well if you're too ill to go to school
You're far too ill to play
But I think you're going to feel a fool
Because today is Saturday.'

Ian Blacklock

Visiting Aus

Way down south
Where the kangaroos live,
Near a place called Marandoo.

I came and strode,
Right down the road,
Playing my didgeridoo.

Up stepped this chap,
With corks in his hat,
Who'd lost his boomerang.

He let it fly,
Up in the sky,
And it hit a caravan.

I caught a bus -
Seeking platypus,
In the river flowing by.

So I sat on a log,
Next to a frog,
When a wallaby caught my eye.

I saw a bear,
Climbing there,
In the boughs of a blue gumtree.

And without any fuss,
I rode the bus,
Back to Perth for tea.

Kevin Whittington

Chickens

There's a house on the hill
Where chickens sit on a sill.
One by one they spread about
Slowly, they don't shout.

Two brown, two white, three sand
In the nettles stand,
They scrape the ground
Food they've found.

Until we open our door,
Sensing something more
They run to the fence
Through weeds, flowers dense.

Remains of our breakfast
Only a minute did it last.
Now, quite content
For that morsel sent.

Their numbers seem depleted
As colours not repeated,
Has anyone seen?
The fox has been,
Feathers scattered on the floor,
Farmer's temper soars.

Rain comes down
Hens disappear and frown
Until it stops
Then heads pop.

Let's now hope
He'll not need a rope
To catch the fox
And in a box
Take him far away
To be kept at bay.
Then the chickens can settle
Once again in the nettle.

Sandra Moran

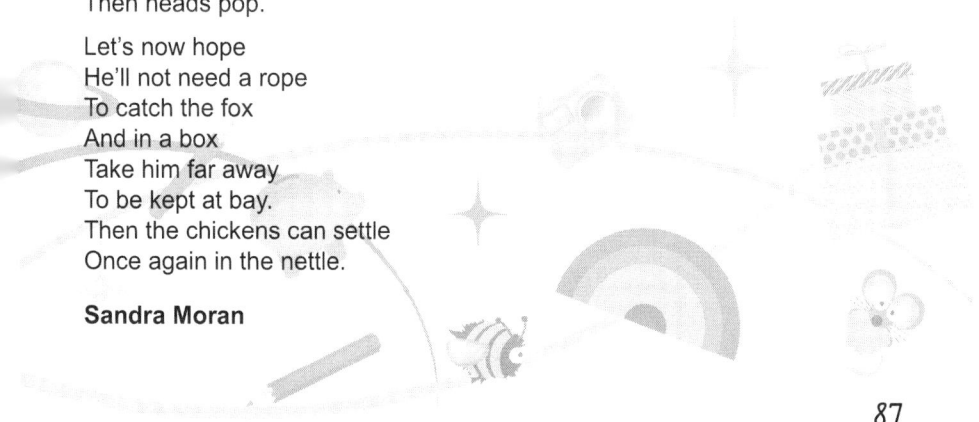

The Bear And The Bunny

Once there was a lonely bear,
Who lived in the land of I-Don't-Care;
Who did what he did
With a shuffle and a shrug,
A tear in his eye,
And a sad old mug;
And every night he said a prayer:
'O where is my own true love, love, love?
O where is my own true love?'

Across the sea in Land-Of-Money,
There lived a beautiful, sad, young bunny;
Who did what she did
With a hop and a sigh,
And a whimper and a tear
In her big blue eye;
And every night - now this is funny -
She also prayed for her true, true love:
'Oh where is my own true love?'

And both their prayers flew up in the sky,
Past the clouds and the moon so high,
Where Someone cared,
And Someone heard;
Who acted on
Their every word,
And brought them together in the By-and-By,
So they could find their love, love, love,
So they each found their own true love . . .

John Bliven Morin

Mama's Bathtime Bubbles

Mama pours the liquid
Into the running bath,
The bubbles start performing
And make the baby laugh.

Ten dance through the window
Nine boogie through the door,
Eight float high in the air
A new world to explore.

Seven bubbles are dancing
There's a carnival in the street,
Six are swinging and swaying
To the happy calypso beat.

Five bubbles big and squeezy
Bounce with the disco groove,
The disco lights are buzzing
Can you see them move?

Four bubbles small and cutey
Are swirling on the ice,
See them whirling with their skates
Watch them turn and slice.

Three bubbles fat and juicy
Are bobbing up and down,
Watch them at the circus
Like the balls of a juggling clown.

Two bubbles white and fluffy
Are floating like a cloud,
One drops in the baby's hand, *pop!*
Baby's laughing loud!

Elayne Ogbeta

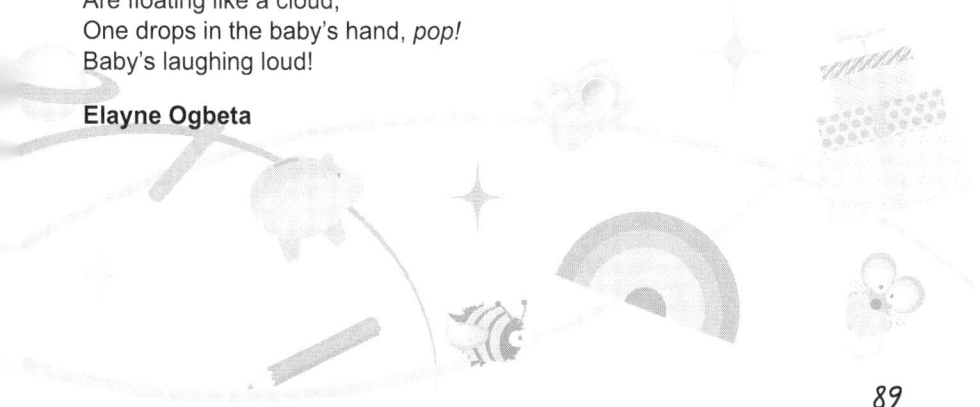

A Wonderful Day

The sun reaches through my window
And gently strokes my face
It is time to get out of bed
Or else for school I'm late
The hawthorns are out, the daffodils too
The birds are chirping happily
The bees are busily making honey
It is a wonderful day to be free
Free from the worries of the less fortunate
Free to walk safely to my school's gate
Free to think whatever I want
Free to pursue my life's ambition
It's a wonderful day to be free.

Yvonne Edwards Scott

Rose's Nose

There was once a girl called Rose Twinkle Toes,
Who had a habit of picking her nose!
She picked until her fingers were sore,
And couldn't even open the door.

One night she found she was in a pot!
And realised she was a blob of snot.
So never again would she pick her nose
What will become of Rose Twinkle Toes?

Megan Pridham

Best Friends

Friends like you match with friends like me,
Rocking as we are you can see,
I and you, you and me, will be best friends for eternity!
Excited as we are about ponies!
Nothing can stop us, even boys, from being best friends,
Don't make this ponytastic friendship end!

Charlotte Stiles

It's Guy Time!

'Please may we have,' the children ask,
'Some newspapers, an empty sack,
Dad's old trousers,
That crumpled hat,
The ruined top
With the ketchup spot
And perhaps some tape
So we can make
These worn-out things
Into a shape?'
You smile as they triumphantly cry,
'Please give a penny for our Guy!'

Debra Dando

What A Spooky Place

The curtains hung in tatters,
The windows were coated in grime,
The weeds were as high as the doorways,
This house was forgotten by time.

The brambles clung to each other,
As they fought for a path to the sun,
A sun that hid in the shadows,
A place where others had run.

T'was a chill in the air that evening,
No surprise, considering its past,
In the Inn, I learnt of its history,
And how no one, past midnight, could last.

A darkness now descended,
As in trepidation I stepped,
Over the threshold that crumbled beneath me,
A place over which others had leaped.

I had heard that jewels could be found here,
Amongst the cobwebs of spiders long dead,
I was told they sparkled in the glow of the moon,
And the rubies were dark and blood red.

The hall had a staircase, quite rotten,
It spiralled to heights unknown,
The shadows were all enveloping,
And now I felt quite alone.

Was it greed that gave me the power,
To venture down corridors of gloom?
Was it unwise to turn the handle of
That only closed door in the room?

Within something glistened and beckoned,
I hankered to go over and see,
What was there, by the chair, that was rocking, but,
I had to go home for me tea . . .

Hilary Ayling

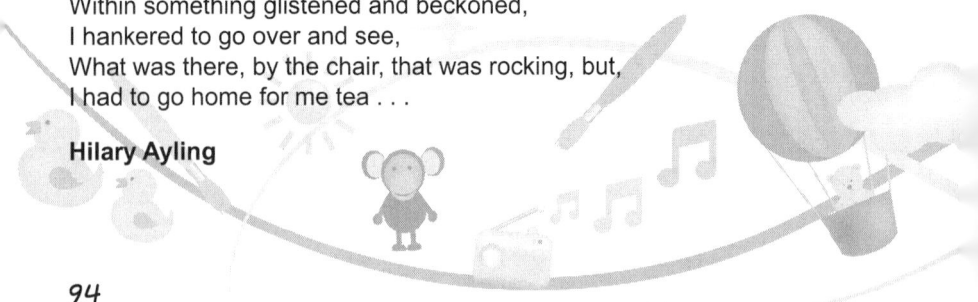

94

My Naughty Brother

That's my brother in that armchair there,
Reading his 'Batman' books,
Curled up warm and cosy
With the heroes, cops and crooks.

Mum's pleased he's gone so quiet now,
Not noisy any more,
'Cos before he started reading
He was leaping round the floor.

The windows were all rattling,
The floorboards shook and cracked,
And when the clock fell off the shelf
Mum landed him a whack!

That set him off a-howling
For a quarter hour at least,
But then he stopped and settled down
And now we've got some peace.

Our dad would smile if he was here
To see him sit so quiet;
Dad's always shouting, 'Sit and read!'
But he doesn't often try it.

Yes, he's calmer than he's been in years,
Since he was ill in bed,
So . . . I think I'll creep behind his chair
And smack him on the head.

Eileen Caiger Gray

The Possum

In a tropical land where the tall trees grow,
Where it rains each day and they never get snow,
There's a small, timid possum that I used to know.
Who lived among the leaves.

From branch to branch he travelled his way,
Only moving by night and never by day,
To find his next meal, then to rest after play,
At home among the leaves.

He awoke with the moon always hiding from light,
To live through the day could damage his sight.
The rays of the sun were always too bright,
Shining among the leaves.

Although he enjoyed his nocturnal land,
He wanted to feel warm light on his hand,
In a clearing below, with no trees, he would stand,
Toes buried in fallen leaves.

Nightly he wandered, not making a sound,
Till one night he slipped and fell to the ground,
Finding himself with grass all around,
No longer among the leaves.

He stumbled along, confused it is said,
(His confusion was caused by a bump on his head),
Only to go where so his feet led,
Treading upon the leaves.

Pushing a path through tightly packed grasses,
Dawn was approaching. Oh my, how time passes,
His eyesight was saved by finding sunglasses,
Lying upon the leaves.

As the sun slowly rose to brighten the wood,
He knew that the light would do him no good,
Till the glasses were put in the place where they should,
He rested with the leaves.

Now the possum is known and is locally famed,
For living by day, and cannot be blamed,
For having his glasses beautifully framed,
Shaped like fallen leaves.

Mark Coram

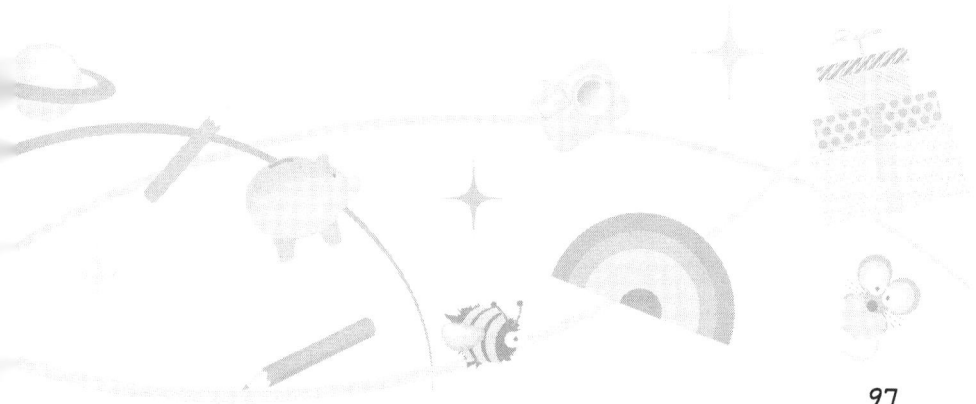

Parent's Revenge

There was a little girl called Codie.
In her nose she found a bogie;
She rolled it round and flicked it far.
It landed on her dad's new car.

When she saw, she laughed out loud
Because she was so very proud,
But then her father came outside
And little Codie ran to hide.

Dad shouted, 'Come on, time for school!
And being late's against the rule!'
As she got in, she hung her head.
Her chubby cheeks turned scarlet red.

'What's the matter love?' asked Dad.
'Are you angry? Are you sad?'
'I'm fine!' she said, and looked away.
She couldn't think of what to say.

Luckily, Dad still hadn't seen
The bogie on the car windscreen,
And as it had begun to rain,
She hoped it'd wash the windowpane.

But across the glass the bogie spread;
It looked like mouldy, soggy bread.
Dad said, 'Oh no! What can it be?
We'll have to stop the car and see.'

Codie had to then admit
Her bogie had been the real culprit,
But Dad stayed calm, gave her a cloth,
And said, 'OK just wash it off.'

Codie's face cringed with disgust.
'All right,' she grumbled, 'If I must!'
Her dad sat back and he just smiled
At the lesson he would teach his child.

The more poor Codie rubbed away,
The more the bogie was there to stay.
In fact, instead of starting to clear,
More and more it began to smear.

The bogie worked like super wax.
It polished the surface and the cracks.
Eventually the whole car was clean;
More than it had ever been!

Codie worked till she was tired;
Her effort was to be admired.
She arrived at school just after break,
Not looking very wide awake.

Her teacher said she was a fool,
For being so very late for school;
And since she didn't pay attention,
Codie got a week's detention!

Codie now carries a hanky round,
Making a noisy trumpet sound.
When she feels a blockage in her nose,
She no longer picks, she blows.

So if, like Codie, you're a wild
Fun-loving, mischievous child,
Please learn a lesson from this tale
Before your bogie lands you in jail!

Melanie Calvert

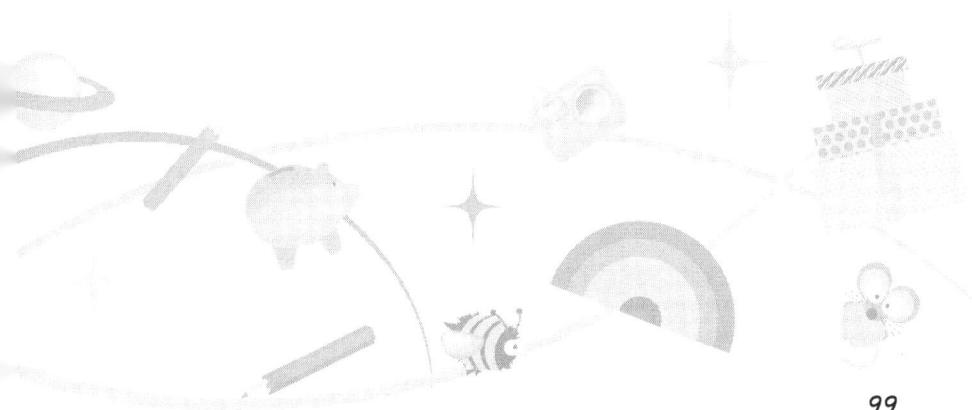

A Special Visitor

That night I couldn't sleep at all
For I was so excited
To think I'd soon be welcoming
The person I'd invited.

It all began in class
When I was not so wide awake
And missed the last instruction
So I made a small mistake

Instead of handing in
My 'Famous Person Invitation'
I had posted off an invite
To the Sovereign of the nation!

But, strange as it may seem,
I got a call from someone posh
To tell me that
'The Queen would love to come for tea and nosh'

Now, news like that is hard
To keep a secret very long
But those I told just thought
I must have heard the caller wrong.

But one more call came through
That even I was shocked to take
Her Royal Highness rang to say
There'd been a royal mistake

The golden carriage had gone in
To have an MOT
So she would have to cycle -
If that was all right with me.

Well, lost for words, I made a grunt,
Her Highness said, 'Hooray!
And I will need to park it
In your bike sheds, if I may'

Yes, this time, they just thought me mad
'He's lost it,' they agreed,
And added; 'It's a visit from a doctor

That you need!'

Until that Thursday morning
As we dreamt our way through science:
We looked outside and spotted
A peculiar appliance

There must have been a hundred wheels
All golden as the sun, and
Fifty saddles of red leather
Lined with diamonds, every one.

And every seat had pedals
Save the centre one alone,
Which sat up high above the rest
And looked more like a throne

And on the throne was perched the Queen
In T-shirt, jeans and crown
And just to look a bit more royal
A fur-lined denim gown

And on the T-shirt, on the front
In velvet, royal blue
Emblazoned were a large ER
And a whopping giant Q!

The six ladies-in-waiting
Flanked her Highness front and back
Each holding clothes or jewellery
In a big black plastic sack.

Then, next to them, with tall fur hats
Sat straight the Queen's own Guard
And, though their faces did not flinch
Their black boots peddled hard

The Beefeaters in costumes fine
And large moustaches too,
Whose whiskers fluttered in the breeze
As bagpipes near them blew!

The Scottish pipers all wore kilts
Of tartans red and green
And this whole lot was quite
The strangest sight you've ever seen!

When Miss Malone caught sight of this
She ran to fetch the Head
But changed her route mid-stride
To go find Union Jacks instead

In seconds there was panic
Like you'll never see again
While Her Majesty dismounted
With her royal maids and men.

The bike sheds weren't designed to take
A royal 50 seater
But, though it did stick out a bit
It fitted, to the metre!

Her Highness and her entourage
Looked round our school for hours
And when she went we thanked her
With a big bouquet of flowers

And as they all rode off again
Her Highness called to me:
'I'm sorry dear, I don't have time
To come to you for tea.'

Of course I did not mind at all
For there amid the crowd
I was a little hero
Who had made the whole school proud!

Jeremy Richards

Findley The Guinea Pig

This is the tale of Findley
A sweet little boy guinea pig
And when we're asleep he is secretly
Planning his next amazing trick
He likes to do somersaults and slides
All over the sofa and chairs
The TV was his first great adventure
But now he starts from the top of the stairs

His first started out with backflips
And then carried on, if he dared
To the dizzing heights of the fridge
But now he's not even that scared
The coat hooks are all part of his act
And the handles are springboards of course
But he always remembers to put back
All the furniture if he stops hearing snores.

Hooray for the amazing Findley Pig
I wish you could see him right now
He's ever so quietly quick
And I'm sure if you did see, he'd bow
He loves all the climbing and crawls
All over the ceiling and chairs
On two legs, his tail and all fours
And he constantly slides down the stairs

So now we must leave him to sleep
He thanks you all for your applause
'Cause it's bed time for this guinea pig
And he's worn out his four little paws.

Ade Horton

The Owl And The Hedgehog

The woods are darkening, the moon is appearing through the branches;
leaves are falling gently and a little hedgehog is humming to himself:

'I am not frightened.
I am scared of no one.

My lunch box is full and I've got a plan:
I can sleep and dine, I've even packed a flan
But home to tea I shall not be coming

Mum said: Don't be a fool and I don't know how . . .
Well it's all her own fault now
And I am not *ever* returning!

I am not frightened.
I am scared of no one.'

'Hello, baby, where are you going?
Asked a large owl posted on a tree stump.
Can we help? Are you lost?'

'I am not frightened.
I am scared of nothing.

Please leave me alone Owl:
Mum and I have had a row
And I am not ever returning.'

'Won't your parents worry?
I may be an old fastidious bird but . . .
What will you do if you're hungry?
The woods are full of danger, you know'

'I am not frightened.
I am scared of no one.

No one will tell me what to do!
I want to do just what I do!'

'And what *do* you do?' asked the owl.

'I run, I'm gone, I'm up for an adventure!
What do *you* do you old vulture?'

'I fly, I dive, I am having a bowl
Of hedgehog soup right now!'
Whistled the owl, and as she said:
She took off in her silent flight and
Wings spread, claws at the ready,
She scooped up the baby.

Why should you go running in the woods and trusting strangers when you could be safely home with the people who love you?

Diane Frost

No Dodos Rap

Everybody knows,
That there ain't no dodos,
No duck-billed platitudes,
Beastly old beautitudes,
Elephants with attitudes,
And no dodos.

Pangolins with long snouts,
Hitchhikers, boy scouts,
Magpies, meat pies,
Clean air, clear skies,
Junk food, French fries,
And no dodos.

Woodpeckers, firewood,
Monday morning feel good,
Real ales, humpback whales,
Full nets, empty jails,
Make a wish when all else fails,
And no dodos.

Letters in the mailbox,
Early morning matched socks,
Rainforest, open spaces,
Open hands, open faces,
Front teeth without braces,
And no dodos.

Leopard seals, rhinos,
Bright eyes, dry nose,
Newspapers door-to-door,
Stop work at ten to four,
Poetry, folklore,
And no dodos.

Green leaves on every tree,
Peace for all eternity,
Friendship, honesty,
Helping hands, sincerity,
People just like you and me,
And . . . no dodos!

Mike Davies

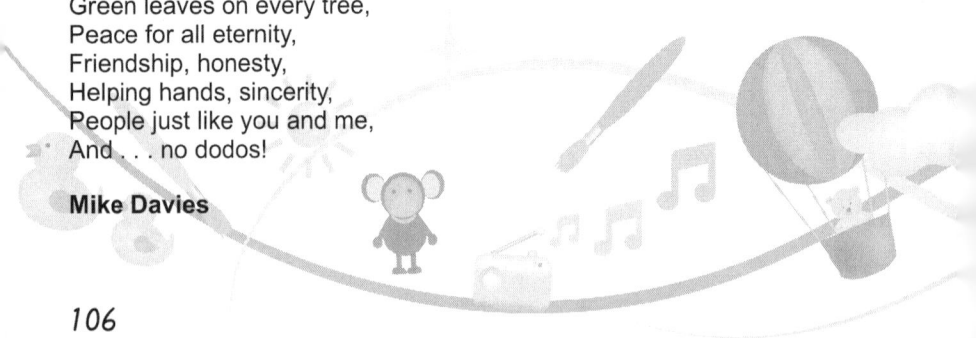

Habits

Picking your nose and sucking your thumb
Chewing your hair and scratching your bum
These are all habits you must try to resist
Because if you don't you'll start to be missed

When being picked for a team you'll be standing alone
They won't want to pick you they'll all start to moan
Because of your habits you'll be pushed to one side
Picked on and bullied with nowhere to hide

So if you want to be cool like 'Ben 10' or 'Bratz'
And you want to be picked for an important match
Ditch those dirty habits and soon you will find
You're trendy and popular and not left behind.

Trudi Collis

Homework

Here's the story of Georgie Tate
Who liked to play and stay up late.
He couldn't read, or write, or calculate
And homework was his greatest *hate!*

He never ever read a book
He thought it boring, so he took
To playing Xbox games
And never learnt his letter names.

He spent each night and all his days
In a *fuzzy, muzzy, wuzzy* haze.
Then one day Georgie saw
A computer game upon the floor.
The pictures were of monsters green
With the sharpest teeth he'd ever seen.
'What do these words say?' Georgie asked
Of anyone who was going past.

His teacher, Miss Hermione Floo
Said, 'Georgie, this will never do!'
'To play this game, you must know
What these words say and where they go.'
She wrote the words upon a card
And Georgie tried, but found it hard.
Georgie took his words off home with him
On a piece of card all long and thin.
He knew it was homework but all the same
He did so want to play that game.

In a very short while to his surprise
He saw a word he *recognised.*
He played his game and sometimes won
And now finds homework
Lots of *fun.*

Carol Humphreys

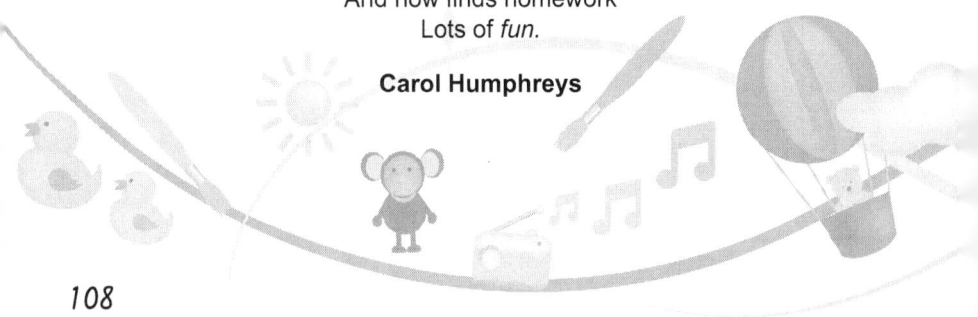

My Teacher The Vampire

Today was very scary,
I really could have cried,
Our teacher was so horrible,
I had to run and hide.
The teacher's teeth had all but gone,
White fangs were there instead,
The blinds were drawn to make it dark,
The teacher's eyes were red.
'I was bitten by a vampire bat,'
Said the teacher, not in jest,
So no more maths or English work,
Today we'll have blood tests.

Leigh Maynard

Bogey Song

When all the monsters are creeping
And the sun has gone to bed.

Up pops a bogey and this is what he said . . .

I'm a dingle dangle bogey with a flippy floppy head,
You can flick me just like this
Or eat me just like that!

Natasha Nicolson

Sock Monster

The sock monster climbs up the waste pipe
And into your washing machine
He'll hide up in a corner
To ensure he can't be seen.
Then when you put your clothes in
And you've set the washer's clock
He'll dive into your washing
And select a single sock.
This special prize he'll carry off
To his secret hidden lair
And share this tasty morsel
With his monster wife so fair.

John Fenn

The Cuddle-Me-Dos

Granny and Grandpa Cuddle-Me-Do
Lived in a posh house near the zoo
They had a dog called Hug-Me-Quick,
Who liked to chase a nice straight stick
To be thrown and scrambled after
Amid peals of laughter.

Granny and Grandpa Cuddle-Me-Do
Belonged to children just like you,
Who were given pocket money once a week
Which they spent at the shops on sweets.
Hug-Me-Quick was a guard dog bold
He kept an eye on the goods that were sold.

Grandpa was known as Cuddles for short.
People said he was quite a sport.
Grandma was his favourite girl.
Her eyes sparkled and her hair it curled.
Grandma baked Cuddles' favourite cake
A cream-filled sponge just for his sake.

Diane Blench

Mary, Mary

Mary, Mary Quite Contrary
Baked a fresh fruit pie
Little Jack Horner was asked to tea
And simply asked her, 'Why?'

Mary, Mary Quite Contrary
Cried, 'Please, just say you'll come,'
Little Jack Horner gave a warm smile
When she said the pie was 'plum'

Little Bo Peep came with the sheep
So did Simple Simon
Jack and Jill came down the hill
And even brought the pieman

Lucy Locket did not come
She could not find her pocket
And this little Piggy lost his way home
Coming back from market

Hickory Dickory looked at the clock
He thought he might be late
So he ran to the end of the garden path
And leapt over the garden gate

Horsey, Horsey, don't you stop
Trotted down the lane with a clipperty-clop
He met Cock Horse along the way
He was ridden by his Lady Gay

Twinkle, Twinkle Little Star
Watched them from the sky
How she envied everyone
Their slice of fruit-filled pie

Old King Cole, the merry old soul
Brought his fiddlers three
He and Mary danced a jig
A sight for all to see

Mary, Mary Quite Contrary,
Gave a contented sigh
'It's good to see so many friends
Enjoying my plum pie.'

Denise Edmonds

Pasty's Best

The pasty's delicious
The pasty is good
The pasty is really
My favourite fud

You don't need a knife
And you don't need a fork
With your mouth full of turnip
It's tricky to talk

Pasties are wonderful
Pasties are great
You don't need to sit
And you don't need a plate

The pasty is perfect
The pasty's complete
It's the best thing to bite
As you walk down the street

The all-in-one meal
You can eat on the run
Forget the unspeakable
Sesame seed bun

Abandon your junk food
And the southern fried bucket
As for the McBurger
You know where you can chuck it

Get your laughing gear
Round a pasty or two
And you'll never want korma
Or hot vindaloo

Cos pasties have pastry
Steak, veggies or cheese
With onion and pepper
(Which may make you sneeze)

They're tasty and faultless
You really can't quibble
They make you feel happy
But don't make you dribble

And now you can eat them
All over the shop
From Penzance to Glasgow
Till your tummy goes *pop!*

In olden days miners
Would throw the last bit
For knockers and pixies
To find in the grit

And woe betide those
Who forgot to throw theirs
Because bad luck would follow
And they'd fall down the stairs . . . (or something!)

They melt in your mouth
Like proverbial butter
They cure aches and pains
And help budgies who stutter

Don't throw them to seagulls
Cos this should be banned
They'll swoop from the roof
And de-pasty your hand

You can't trust a seagull
But you *can* trust a pasty
They'll never upset you
Or even turn nasty

So let's all now drink
To the world's greatest pie
Three cheers for the pasty
Shout, 'Hip, hip, hooriye!'

Robert Barratt

The Mouse Trap

In a field, near a lake,
Lives a mouse, his name is Jake.
Jake is relatively well
But Jake's been through all kinds of hell.
It all began one winter's day,
The air was cold (it wasn't May),
The fog was thick, the lake was ice,
These weren't great times for field mice.

As Jake was seeking stuff to eat
Through the mist with freezing feet,
He noticed, much to his surprise,
The earth beneath him start to rise.
He quickly scurried out the way
As soil and mud and rocks did spray
In all directions from this strange mound.
Jake made his way to firmer ground.

Looking back from where he'd fled,
He saw two eyes, a nose, a head.
Such a creature he had never known
(Jake didn't get out much on his own)
He wanted answers straight and true
So bravely squeaked, 'Er . . . who are you?'
Replied the creature, 'Please don't fret,
I am a mole, I'm glad we've met!'

'You've got to help me Mr Mouse
Some monstrous thing has wrecked my house
We've got to catch it, that's my goal
Quick, follow me back down this hole.'
Jake had hoped he would get some food
But it's not like rodents to be rude
As the mole went back to whence it came,
Jake grit his teeth and did the same.

Thinking less of food and more of fear
Jake couldn't see, he couldn't hear
His faithful nose was all he had
'Twas a good thing this mole smelled bad.
He pursued the mole for mile on end
Slope after slope, bend after bend
Jake was wishing he'd not taken flight
When at the tunnel's end, he saw the light.

They both emerged the worse for wear,
The mole pointed through the icy air,
Jake saw a sorry looking mess,
It was the mole's recent address.
His house was crushed, his home destroyed,
No wonder he was so annoyed.
Jake asked him, 'Who on Earth did that?'
The mole revealed, 'It was a cat!'

'A cat?' mused Jake, 'What's one of those?'
'It has whiskers growing from its nose
Its teeth are sharp, its claws are long
And it hates mice,' the mole went on.
'Hates mice!' cried Jake with dread and fear
'Why then did you bring me here?'
'I'll tell you why, you are the bait
Now would you please sit here and wait?'

Protested Jake, 'I am good-willed
But if I sit here, I will be killed.'
'Mr Mouse, you will not be deceased
I've the perfect plan to catch this beast
I promise you, you'll be OK
Will you help me out? What do you say?'
Jake who was noble, kind and good,
Nodded his head and said he would.

So Jake sat still, as bait should be,
With the mole in close proximity
And it wasn't long before that cat
Crept towards where Jake was sat
But just as it was set to pounce,
The mole appeared and did announce,
'Revenge is sweet, you feline thug'

And pushed it in the hole he'd dug.

Jake and the mole had caught their foe
What happened next, you need not know
Suffice to say, cats now think twice
Before upsetting moles or mice.
After words of gratitude and praise
Both creatures went their separate ways.
Jake's since decided, much too late,
Come winter he will hibernate.

Ed Harris

The Truth About Goldilocks

My name is Goldilocks - you might know me . . .
I went into the house of the three bears,
This is a poem explaining myself.
Explaining just how I ended up there.

The door was left wide open,
What option did I have left?
Walk past and let the house get burgled?
The house was in danger of theft!

So I went inside to check it out,
To see if everything was okay,
It would only be for a minute,
I wasn't planning to stay . . .

Alright . . . I had a bit of porridge,
But breakfast is the most important meal!
My mother always tells me so,
I never intended to steal!

And okay I broke Baby Bear's chair,
I was just having a little rest,
I was simply waiting till the bears got back,
I was doing what I thought was best!

And lastly I went to the three bears' beds,
Just to check they weren't still asleep,
But all this helping the bears had me exhausted,
So I popped into bed without a peep.

But when the bears came back they went mad!
And before I could explain,
They chased me right out of the cottage,
All my hard work was in vain!

So you see I never meant to upset them.
What else was I to do?
I was just being a good neighbour of course!
You believe me - don't you?

Natalie Foley

My Week

Monday is for monsters under the bed.
Tuesday is for chewing, chocolate and sweets.
Wednesday is for working, I must show willing.
Thursday is for friends and tea.
Friday is for fighting, with pillows of course!
Saturday is for playing
Sunday is for sleeping ready for Monday.

Clare Todd

The White Teddy Bear

There it sat, alone, in the shop window,
Pure white like unmarked snow,
No ether colour on its coat in sight,
With tiny, little button eyes,
As black, as black as coal,
Its mouth seemed to smile,
A biding for any child,
To come in to kiss and hold,
For a hug and cuddle tight,
And dream of while asleep at night,
But the sign said this bear is not for sale,
it was only to be used for display,
Not a toy for fun and games or play,
Many a child filled with dismay,
As parents lead them off as they cried,
A tear would drop from the bear's eye.
And it would lift its paw to wave,
A sad and silent goodbye.

Pauline Uprichard

The Little Stinky Pig

Stinky Pig went out one day, a happy pig was he
With Chalkey White the crocodile and Bumble Bong the bee
'There is a place in Africa that I can take you to,'
Said Chalkey White the crocodile, to make you smell like new
Along they went together to the land of silky green
Trees were full of coconuts, the grass was nice and clean
Piggy met the Ju Ju man who came to cast his spells
Dancing 'round his jellypot to drive away the smells
Ju Ju went to Piggy and he put him in the pot
He sat him on the fire until the pig was nice and hot
'I think you want to eat me,' cried the piggy, 'let me go'
'Oh no,' replied the crocodile and licked his lips just so
'Oh help me,' cried the piggy to Bumble Bong the bee
'The crocodile and Ju Ju man are cooking me for tea!
So Bumble stung the Ju Ju man and piggy ran away
Over went the jellypot on crocodile, *hooray!*
Now Piggy's very happy and he couldn't give a fig
'And I don't care if I'm smelly,' said the little stinky pig.

Norman Flint

Larry Liked A Cake Or Two!

Larry was a llama
He had a motorbike
He crashed it at a roundabout
And so he bought a trike

He didn't use a helmet
But had a splendid view
Because of his long neck of course
While riding he would chew

For if you see a llama
They chew for hours and hours
I'm not sure what they're chewing on
But think they like wild flowers

Soon Larry's trike was famous
He even made the news
They filmed him at the racetrack
And scything through some queues

He rides around the country
And sometimes stops for tea
He likes a cuppa with some cake
And that's where he met me

We shared a pleasant afternoon
Once he pulled up his chair
He chewed on a vanilla slice
While I munched my éclair!

But all too soon the cake had gone
And Larry said farewell
His trike it roared as he set off
To where, well who can tell?

So if you hear a trike nearby
Its engine deep and gruff
Hold out a cuppa and some cake
Cos Larry likes the stuff!

Think once, think twice, think llama
Each time you see a bike
It could be my friend Larry
The llama with the trike!

John Dodds

Goblins

Deep in the shadows
Near the true edge of time,
Live two little goblins
In a world filled with rhyme.

They run through the forest
With rabbits and squirrels,
And sing to the treetops
As they tumble and twirl.

In the heart of this forest
Lives a little old witch
Who loves these two goblins
Called Jenni and Mitch.

She teaches them magic
With fireworks and song,
And sings to the wizard
Who brings them along.

To his castle of willow
Set deep in the ground,
Where beetles and spiders,
Work hard all night long.

And when comes the morning
All goblins must sleep.
No trace can be found
Of this world of the deep.

Josephine Duthie

Porky Pies

I can't get out of bed Mum,
It happened in the night.
A monster tied me to the posts,
It gave me quite a fright!

I can't go to school Mum,
A squirrel stole my shoes.
He did it to the neighbours too,
I heard it on the news!

I can't visit Granny Mum,
My bike is in the tree,
A swarm of bees came swooping down
And snatched it off of me!

I can't do my homework Mum,
I lost it on my walk
A magpie grabbed it from my hands
And ate it with a squawk!

I can't tidy my room Mum,
I can't get through the door.
A spider came and stole my key
Then crept under the floor!

I can't eat this cabbage Mum,
It makes your toes fall off!
It happens when you blow your nose
And every time you cough.

I can't brush my teeth Mum,
I haven't got a brush.
I dropped it in the toilet
And a monkey pulled the flush!

I can't go to bed Mum,
Daddy never lies.
He said those monsters get you
If you're telling porky pies!

Debbie Hollingdrake-White

Laura Was A Llama

Laura was a llama
With very fluffy hair.
She lived in a zoo
In the middle of the city
On a patch of green grass
Behind some tall iron bars,
And sometimes she got lonely.

But there was one thing
That she looked forward to:
Every Saturday she had a visitor,
A little girl called Milly.
Milly was five years old
And had big blue eyes
And whenever she saw Laura
Out would come her big smile.
Cos Milly loved Laura, you see,
She loved her fluffy fur,
She loved her wobbly knees,
And most of all she really loved
To see her crooked white teeth
When Laura the llama
Grinned at little Milly.

'Look Mummy!' laughed Milly,
Pointing at her furry friend,
'Laura is smiling at me!'
Her mummy chuckled and said:
'Animals don't smile Milly,
Don't be silly.'

But Milly knew better.
She waved at Laura the llama,
And blew her a kiss.
And Laura winked at the girl
As she chewed on her grass.
I've got a little human friend, she thought
I'm such a lucky llama.

Alex Dixon

Tooth Fairy

If your tooth is wobbly
And your gum feels soft and knobbly
Try and pull it out
And shake it all about
If that doesn't work
Bite an apple, let it jerk
And out your tooth will come
Your gum will feel real numb
Place it in a tissue
Your tooth will say, 'I'll miss you'
The tooth fairy's necklace it will join
And then she'll leave you a shiny new coin.

Anne-Marie Howard

Hungry Mouse

I know a nice young lady,
Who went to see her mum,
When she got home she had a shock,
A mouse had attacked the fridge, by gum.

The poor little mouse was hungry,
He wanted something to eat,
How could he open the door?
He was sure he could not be beat.

The mouse he had a brainwave,
I'll nibble the seal on the door,
Then creep through the hole I've made,
Food, he wanted some more and more.

He got inside the fridge,
Eating a bit of this and that,
Then a thought came into his head,
Does the lady have a cat?

Luckily for the mouse,
The lady had no cat,
So he kept on eating,
A bit of this and that.

At last the mouse was full,
He'd been eating all day,
So he squeezed out through the hole,
And quickly ran away.

Jeff Northeast

Dandelion Success

(From 'The Planet Mars Book of Earth Sciences', fact number, 4,754,309)

Like the birds and the bees spread the flowers and the trees,
So the human child spreads the dandelion weed.
That's the dandelion weed with the dragon-back leaf
And the lollipop head of a thousand seeds.

How he does the deed:
Well he shakes and he throws and he puffs and he blows.
Seeds can end up in the mouth, even right up the nose
(This may cause a sneeze - that's a nasal breeze - to reverse the flow).

And if that doesn't do it
Then he'll nominate a patch and charge right through it
Just kicking and flicking and whacking with his toes.
But whatever the deed thus the seed is freed and away it goes.

So a brief recap:
They're blown and thrown and booted, so sown,
So those tatty yellow heads just spread and grow.
(What the child gets back is not as known fact, meaning -
Who on Earth knows?)

Janine-Langley Wood

Play Centre

His mother had done her best to keep his mind
on the painting they'd started together,
but his pallid nostrils twitched, lifted up,
sensed something in the air, or on her face.

Scuttling through a gap in the giggling fence
of other children huddled round the hutch,
he found it easy to slip the catch, and run,
his head hidden by the long tall grass
that she had kept on saying should be green,
to the rabbit-hole, where he'd not be caught.

Clawing down the apple-crumble tunnel,
he wasn't sorry he'd screamed this morning
as she tried to cut his sharp bunny-nails.
The burrow had that nest-of-arms smell like
when she was warm-straw in her happy-dress.

No, he didn't envy Ben's thick coat of fur:
it was good for burying your face in
and for drying your cheeks while your fingers
gurgled in the soft-water of his floppy ears,
till the owl-ringed weariness floated from your eyes,
gliding down into Ben's dark vigil of honesty:
animal truth that wouldn't blink or look away,
a sky-darkness you could sleep in now, soft-centred
like the kangaroo-pocket your bedroom used to be.

'Come on darling,' He could see Daddy's
twinkling stars much more clearly now,
'Come on love,' all around him bright,
like all the nicest smiles he'd ever known.
'I wish my name was Ben.'
'It's time to go,
Daddy will look after your painting.'
His mother lifted him up, stroked his hairless head.
'The nice doctor's waiting.
Ben will still be here next time.'

And another time . . . But this time,
going home, clawing up the apple-crumble tunnel
into the bright, starry night outside,
we blinked, looked away and gently cried.

Gerald Parker

Wasn't Me

We have a stranger in our house, he comes and leaves a mess
My mum would like to find him, cos he causes lots of stress

He messes up my bedroom, he leaves coats upon the floor
He brings in muddy footprints and he slams and bangs our door.

Mum's hunting for this person living in our house.
We don't know what he looks like, he could even be a mouse.

But every time a mess is made, usually before tea,
When asked who made this dreadful mess, we all say wasn't me!

Let's find this thing called Wasn't Me and bring him to explain
Why all this mess is left about, he really is a pain!

So search we do and do you think we ever seem to find
This person who's called Wasn't me. We're always far behind

But one day Mum assures us, he'll leave us all alone
I expect that day will be the day my children have all flown!

Claire Holder

Magic

Out in the world among mysteries vast
Stories remind us of things that have passed
Things often forgotten as people get older
Are still there to find for those who are bolder

Sometimes dragons will swoop and glide through the air
Though can be quite shy so we don't know they're there
Some fairies and pixies still live on the breeze
But rather than us, prefer talking with trees.

Elves still roam free over valleys and ridges
While trolls can sometimes be found under bridges
Frogs turn into princes almost every day
But prefer not to do it out on full display

Because you don't see them, doesn't mean they're not there
Even princesses in towers that let down their hair
So wherever you are and wherever you go
Please try to remember there is more to this show

Many colourful strands in life's rich weave
So open your mind, set your heart to believe
Some things in our lives can be truly tragic
But the worst of them all is forgetting the magic.

Anthony Green

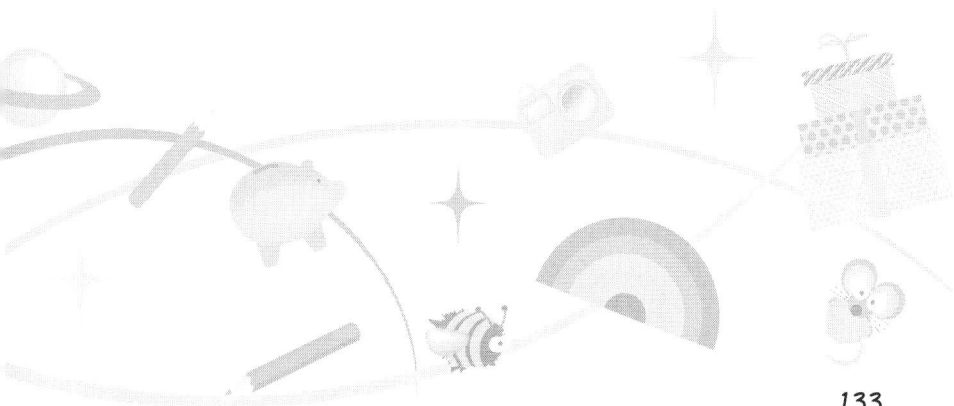

Teddy's Adventures

Begin at the beginning
A fresh start
Teddy, happy and free
Worldly wise 'Teddy Love'
Nice work
Welcome back Teddy
To the schoolroom
Essentials at the window seat
Leaving on a jet plane
Teddy jet-sets everywhere
Up high in the sky
Lots of books in the reading room
Teddy adventures
Lovely stories, shopping,
Our esteemed guest sighs!
Teddy on holiday in Europe!

Stella Thompson

Professor Backward

I shall always go backward
I shall be Professor Backward
And never go forward again

I shall rise at night
And retire at dawn
I shall water the carpet
And hoover the lawn

I'll wear short pants in winter
And a fur coat when it's hot
I will cook in a glass
And drink from a pot

I will wear my pyjamas all day
And my best suit to bed
With my hat on my feet
And my shoes on my head

And I will say goodbye
When I mean hello
Though this is ever so silly
I know . . . I know

But I will always go backward
I shall do everything in reverse
Until you say you love me
And kiss away my curse.

Scott Nell

Christmas Eve

Lying in bed and trying to sleep
When all we want to do is creep
Downstairs to see what Santa's brought
But we're afraid we might get caught
Because Mum told us that we must stay
In bed until it's Christmas Day.
So, we imagine Santa way up high
Riding his sleigh across the sky
Loaded with lots of presents and toys
Delivering them to all the girls and boys.
But it's getting late and will soon be light
So we snuggle down with eyes shut tight
And slowly we drift off to sleep
Dreaming of presents while counting sheep.

Stella Mortazavi

Night-Time

When it's dark and we go to bed,
The nocturnal animals come out instead,
There's Mr Bat, he can't see
All of a sudden *bang*, he smacks right into a tree,
And Mr Owl, he flies through, making lots of noise, *tu-whit tu-whoo*
Mr Fox is sleek and sharp, dashing through the night.
Bumps into Mr Badger, which gives him such a fright,
So when you go to bed and switch off the light,
Remember all the nocturnal animals that come out at night.

Brenda Moran

My Child

Mummy's sorry, she left she needed a rest
I walk with you and you know I do
When you're asleep our secrets you keep
In dragons' realms we do go not too fast
But slow savour the moments we have
Never feel blue, I'm looking out for you
With my special friend
I sent you
Because in her heart
She knew at the start how I felt
When she looked at me
The sadness she could see
And I knew she had a gift
Beautiful child of mine
Come sit by my side
Let's be like dragons and fly
People with tears in their eyes
Just look to the sky
And you will see me smiling away
On a bright moonlit day
Search and you will find
I will be in your mind
When times are tough and fill you with love
Sorry I had to leave, I'm missing home
But I'm with the gifted one
Wherever she goes I come.

Linda Bevan

The Isle Of Ish Crí (Villan(onsens)elle)

While Cringledums flit round the Isle of Ish Crí
The party's begun for Prince Parglimp the third
And Floppletop townsfolk munch fleeples for tea

'Neath moonlight of purple the blimbles run free
Their pepper-specked shrieks sound distinctly absurd
While Cringledums flit round the Isle of Ish Crí

Moombolian mothers pick nisps from the tree
While prayers are intoned for the Fragglesnip bird
And Floppletop townsfolk munch fleeples for tea

There's no school for snimps if you're still under three
(Their language is made up of just one small word)
While Cringledums flit round the Isle of Ish Crí

In spite of the lack of a frumbletop tree
The song of a willabee's never been heard
And Floppletop townsfolk munch fleepies for tea

It's night now and high time, I'm sure you'll agree
For snipperfly fathers to have the last word
While Cringledums flit round the Isle of Ish Crí
And Floppletop townsfolk munch fleepies for tea.

Amanda Hyatt

Waiting For The Bus

I was waiting at the bus stop
For bus thirty-four
But when it finally reached me
The driver said, 'No more!'

'I've picked up so many passengers
They're hanging out the door
Some are sitting three to a seat
Or squashed upon the floor.

I've got old Mavis Trotter
Who's been out to get her tea
She's bought up half the supermarket
And needs six seats you see.

And then the United football team
Are crammed across the back
The coach keeps blowing his whistle
As he swings from the luggage rack.

Old Dr White would like to walk
But his patients live far and wide
His aching knees are terrible
And put him off his stride.

He's on his way to visit
A Mrs Hyacinth Green,
Cos her son Fred has chicken pox
And the largest spots you've seen.

Then there's the local ballet school
Pirouetting in the aisle
Today they're starring in a show
With their teacher Miss Ima V Agile

I mustn't forget Mrs Eggerton Pink
Whose car has broken down
She's taking her six St Bernards dogs
To the vets at the end of town.

And then of course, Bob and Ethel
Who are off to get married in church
But their limo hasn't turned up

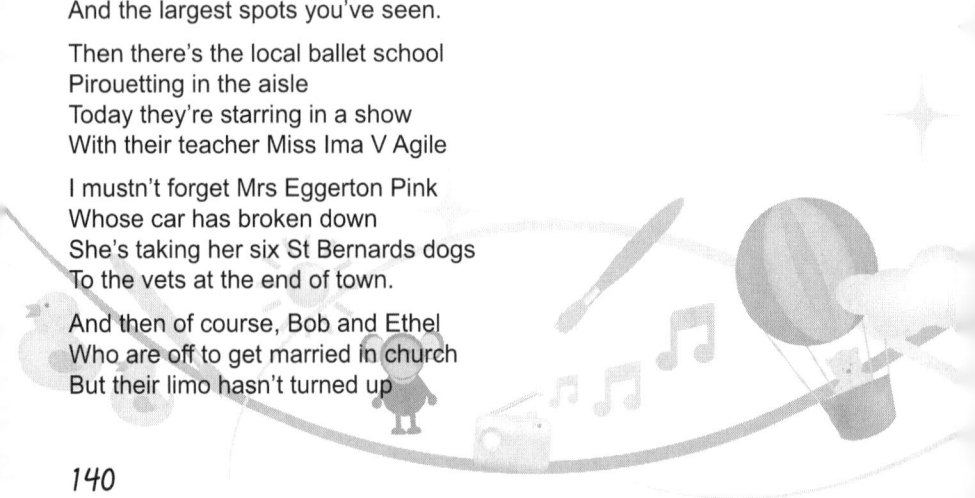

And has left them in the lurch

And finally there's the boat club
Who are on a weekend trip.
They've bought their oars and compasses
To help them steer their ship.

And so you see we have no room
So please don't make a fuss
Cos if you wait just a little while
There'll soon be another bus.

Philippa Rae

Margery

The police have issued a warning
There's an uplift in larceny
There's a one woman crime wave
And her name is Margery

Now Margery is tiny
Her profile is always low
She could be sitting in your pocket
And you wouldn't even know

She says she is a psychic
She says she talks to the dead
She says she has a message
From departed Uncle Fred.

He says that money is evil
He says you've to change your ways
He says, 'Give all your stuff to Margery'
Then she sells it on Ebay.

This little conniving con artist
Won't stop at all your stuff
She'll empty all your bank accounts
She can never get enough

She'll invoke the spirits
And say they're not at rest
She'll take the shirt right off your back
Then come back for your vest

So be alert and on the look out
For master criminal Marge
And heed this simple warning
Small medium at large.

Mark Niel

The Worm Turned

I wouldn't like birds
If I were a worm
I wouldn't like magpies
Or wrens

I'd have to be firm
If I were a worm
And tell them
We'd never be friends

I wouldn't like cats
If I were a bird
I wouldn't like Siamese
Or Blue

I'd soon spread the word
If I were a bird
That a friendship
Just never would do

I wouldn't like dogs
If I were a cat
I wouldn't like shepherds
Or mutts

And that would be that
If I were a cat
No maybes, no ifs,
And no buts.

I wouldn't like worms
If I were a dog
I know 'cause I
Had them last week

I leapt like a frog
As I jiggled and jogged
And I wiggled and squirmed
Cheek to cheek.

Jackie Hosking

Fourth Of July Party

We've sent the word
To the whole of the jungle
You crazy creatures
Get ready to rumble

It's the fourth of July
And we're ready to swing
Get down and get sassy
Come and do your thing

Don't get snooty with me
You spotty-faced cheetah
Get on the dance floor
And move those feetah

Hey Lion dude
Get outta your rut
Swing them shoulders
And jiggle that butt

Now Monkey man
Is a real mean swinger
He's a disco diva
And a beautiful singer

Hey there Snake
You piece of sly
Stop looking at Mouse
With your hungry eye

The hippos are swinging
They're treading that mud
They're looking like dancing
Is right in their blood

I'm Zebediah Zakariah
And I'm here in case of fire
So show me the hose
You dozy crows

I'm a spud on a horse
And I'm looking for the sauce
Barbecue or tomato
Will do this hot potato

Hey Rhino boy
You're doing the stomp
Whoa look out boys
He's ready to romp

Now I'm a real cool bear
And I got funky hair
I don't mean to be rude
But show me to the food

Put some oil in my joints
You slippery oinks
This giraffe can move
Just watch my groove

This elephant ain't fat
You foolish cat
But if I come down there
I'll squash you flat

Listen out for this bird
I'm the best you ever heard
The drums are my dream
You can keep the tambourine

Come on now you guys
Get on the dance floor
Parade that hoof
And shift that paw.

Elizabeth Crompton

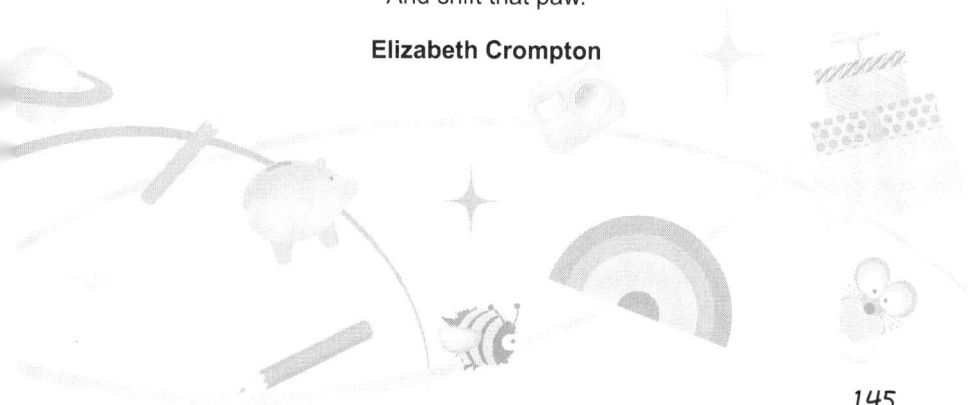

Globe Trotting

So you're halfway round the moon
and heading for Mars
chasing an angel
driving a methane-powered star.
You're laughing at the notion
that you've made it this far,
by the self-propelling motion
of your bed-mobile car

For seven nights now,
it's been go, go, go . . .
exploring new places
at fast, fast, slow . . .
You've learnt so much about geography
your teacher is amazed
when you tell her of continents,
straight-faced, unfazed.

Bedouins don't like camel milk
but it's all they've got to drink.
How the Inuit use a borehole
instead of a kitchen sink.
That lakes on the moon are empty
and Mars is dry, dry dust
and Antarctica is melting
so much that we must

stop using tumble dryers,
turn off the electric light,
get up only when the sun shines,
fight the eco-friendly fight.
Recycle at the bottle bank,
cycle to school,
take a shower, fill the oven up
follow the golden 'green' rules

1: Insulate your home
2: Turn down the thermostat
3: Decide to buy much less
4: Eat organic, curb the fat
5: Teach you friends and neighbours all to do the same
and make sure your rocket engines
are just in dreams and games.

Nancy Charley

Merlin From Berlin

Merlin from Berlin
Went for a ride
Where he was going
He couldn't decide

He went past the school
He went past the shop
And past the lady
Selling lollipops

'Oh,' said Merlin
'I want some sweets.'
And leapt off the bus
Right on to the street

He bought sticky toffee
And ate it quick
And five minutes later
He felt awfully sick

'Oh,' said the lady
Making a fuss
'Never eat sweets
When you're in a rush'

Merlin went home
And as he closed the door
Said, 'I'll never eat sweets fast anymore!'

Jennifer James

My First Day

Today is my first day at school and I can't wait to start.
In my new shirt, tie and blazer, I look so very smart
I'm feeling so excited, I can't wait to make new friends
I hope that when they mark my books I get 10 out of 10.

We left the house at 10 to 9, worried we'd be late.
We hurried up the street and had just got to the gate
When we heard the bell ring and had to form a line
So we'd only just got to the school in the nick of time.

We're now sitting in the classroom, all quiet and still
We've all been given paint pots that we've been asked to fill
By the sink we have been told to form a little queue
Then our teacher tells us the next thing we should do.

She says we should sit down and not move and run about
I'm very pleased that I've been asked to hand the paper out
I walk around the classroom, passing out paper and pens
To all the other children that I hope will be my friends.

I've drawn a lovely picture that I'm told is very neat
And I'm told that I can take it home, as it is mine to keep
The bell has just been rung and we can now go out to play
I really like my school - I'm having so much fun today.

After lunch when I was learning some arithmetic
A rather naughty boy, a piece of paper he did flick
Right across the classroom - it landed on the floor
The teacher asked him kindly not to do it anymore.

We thought it rather funny - it caused such a giggle
When a boy stood in our classroom and did a little piddle
The teacher changed his clothes and told him everything was fine
She told him not to worry - it happened all the time.

Well now the day's come to an end and I am rather sad
I think this is the best day that I have ever had
I walked across the playground kicking at a stone
Then looked up and saw my mummy who had come to take me home.

Marlene Robinson

The Journey Of A Chicken

In a farmyard of Lublicock's land,
Where the land is of water and the sea of sand,
A small chicken Tilly, whom all thought to be silly.
Wanted to fly in the sky, among the clouds high!

'Oh stupid fool!' they all said,
'Like the sky is never under the bed,
Hens can never fly! Foolish feathers!'
'Still tell me!' said Tilly.
'So silly! Then you'll have to go
Through the dark forests of Sickenlo
Where the wicked servants of Sickenlo
The Grumpensteins and Growlipests grow!
Where trees come and eat small chicks,
And basilisks turn you to bricks!'

'But isn't it true, oh Granny and Mummy!
That after the forests are the Snowlifer hills!
Where fairies dance on a full-moon night!
And tell chickens the secret of flight!
Where the dew that rests on Laughter-grass
Can give you happiness that forever lasts!
Where angels and elves, where spirits and jinn
Give you a crown joygold, incense and myrrh?'

The oldies nod, but tell her then
'Do as we say else we don't know when,
Foxes and wolves and witches on sticks
Will roast you in fire and evil Bondiwicks
Will eat your curry, with cardamoms mixed!'

Still she didn't listen to them and took the sword
Of good King Dove and crossed Lazyville's ford
And through the dark, walked as bravely as she could,
Through Grumpenstein's lands and Growlipest's woods!
But by some magic, the monsters ran
From her path, so that those lands
Were at last freed, from Sickenlo's hands!

She went to Snowlifer hills!
And wow! Oh my!

What she saw!
Full of wonder and awe!

For the snow on Snowlifer glistened in light!
And winds spoke to her, the secrets of flight!
And fairies and Jinn, and elves and sprites
Danced around her on each full-moon night!

When she returned flying,
From Snowlifer's peaks, crying.
'Hello chickens and hens!'
The chickens were filled with shame.
'Oh Tilly, we were so silly!
Like Boringville's lord and dame!
Teach us, then, the mystery of flight
So even we may bathe in the new dawn's light!'

So she did and so Lublicock's land,
Was filled with flying hen.
Who flew all day in sunlight or rain.
For flying is such a joy! In Bildigock's name!
And so, in Lublicock's land, across the sea of sand,
Is this history told of Tilly, mighty chicken-heart,
Who taught us flying - the greatest of all art.

Samya Rakshit

Billy Bob's Dilemma

Billy Bob sat frowning,
Schooldays had begun.
He would rather be cavorting through the branches,
That was far more fun.

But sit he must and learn his letters,
Such a puzzle one and all,
Then suddenly, within his ear, he heard
Elfin voices quietly changing, explaining all.

A for the acorns on the bough, B for the berries tasty and sweet,
Oh what a treat to eat.
C for the cats that hiss and fight, D for dogs that howl all night.
E for the eagles soaring high, F for the fox sneaky and sly.

G for the gannet ever eating, H for the hare madly leaping,
I for insects crawling about, J for the Jay shrieking the news about.
K for kittens ever playful, L for the linnet chirpy and cheerful.

M is for mother wise and gay, N is for nanny dozing all day.
O is for ostrich with his head in the sand, P is for the pelican one legged he
stands.
Q for the questioner who must be obeyed, if you know this rhyme you need
not repent.

R is the robin with his glowing redbreast; S is for swans sleek and white,
gliding the waterways, by day and by night.
T is the tawny owl who's wise in the head, U is the umpire who's shaking his
head.

V is for vultures that eat the dead meat; W is for the weasel that thinks lying
is neat.
X stands for the cross when you get things wrong, Y is for yawn, why is this
lesson taking so long?

Z is for Zzzzz as one falls into dreams, oh to be a squirrel up in the trees,
leaping about, happy and free, Billy Bob's dilemma is so easy you see.

Jane Dyson

Catch Of The Day

For many a year there have been strange tales
Of beautiful mermaids with sequin-like scales
And many fishermen have sat and recalled
A flash of something peculiar as the nets are being hauled
Princesses of the sea not knowing if they're friend or foe
Bobbing corks, the boats they look to them, as they watch from deep down below
But stranger still as a tall tale goes
Of an old salty sea dog who once stood up and proposed
'You talk of what you might have seen but I have caught a mermaid and she was eloquent indeed.
Just off the headland of Bantry Bay, up popped her head and I heard her say,
'For many a year the sea we have shared, if you would be so kind I would like to be spared
And in return for your kindness I will gladly repay by bringing fresh fish by the boat load every single day.'
'Sit down you old fool,' the rest of the crew replied
But our salty sea dog just smiled with a glint in his eye
And so the stories are still told, passed down from father to son
About our old salty sea dog's good fortune, and the deal that was done.

Stuart Severn

The Worm

The worm lost its wriggle, he didn't know where.
Maybe inside an apple or even a pear.
The last time he had it was yesterday noon.
He'd be in real big trouble if he didn't find it soon.
With daylight approaching and birds looking round
For their breakfast, he needed to be underground.
For now he was safe, or as safe as could be,
But he must lie quite still, or else they would see
This fat juicy worm, (for he'd put on some weight)
So he really must hide, before it was too late.
He tried to remember, what he did yesterday,
And the reason his wriggle had gone right away.
The last place he'd been, was inside a plum
When it fell off the bush, now he really felt glum.
There was the plum, he could see it quite clear.
But was it too far away? That was his fear.
He rolled over and over and after an hour,
He got to the plum, though it took all his power.
He lay there and rested, then looked all around
To see if his wriggle was there on the ground.
Next he looked up and then gave a shout.
The end of his wriggle was just poking out
Of the hole in the plum, he could see it quite plain,
But how could he get it back to him again?
Just then a slight breeze, gently turned the plum round,
And his wriggle fell out right there on the ground.
'I'll soon put that back,' said the worm with delight,
'Then I'll wriggle myself down a hole out of sight.'

David H Worsdale

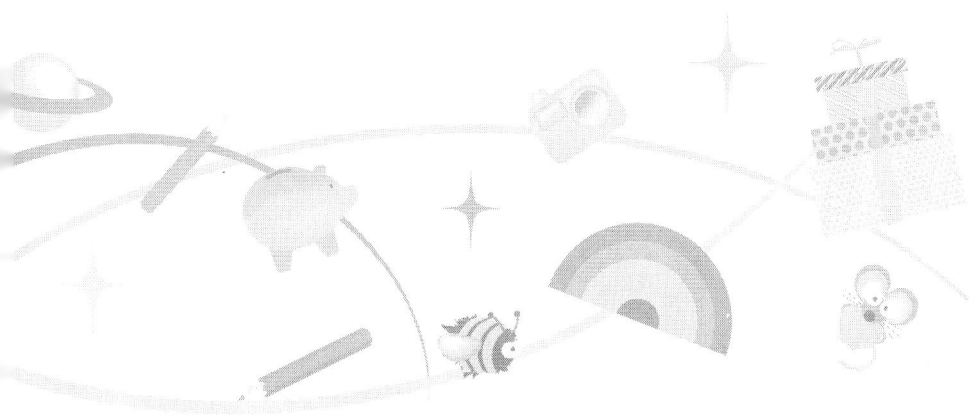

Forward Press Information

We hope you have enjoyed reading this book - and that you will continue to enjoy it in the coming years.

If you like reading and writing poetry drop us a line, or give us a call, and we'll send you a free information pack.

Alternatively if you would like to order further copies of this book or any of our other titles, then please give us a call or log onto our website at www.forwardpress.co.uk

Forward Press Information
Remus House
Coltsfoot Drive
Peterborough
PE2 9JX
(01733) 890099